AF552680

Vodafone salutes the women of substance
– a woman of power, of inspiration, and of radiance.

SHOWCASE
Roli Books
A Roli Books imprint for titles sponsored by individuals or organizations.

Book Concept, Layout, and Design, Roli Books Pvt Ltd
Cover Design, Sneha Pamneja

Published in India by Roli Books
M-75, Greater Kailash II Market, New Delhi 110048, India
Phone + 91 11 4068 2000 **Fax** + 91 11 2921 7185
Email info@rolibooks.com **Web** rolibooks.com

ISBN: 978-81-7436-968-0
Printed and bound at
Thomson Press, New Delhi

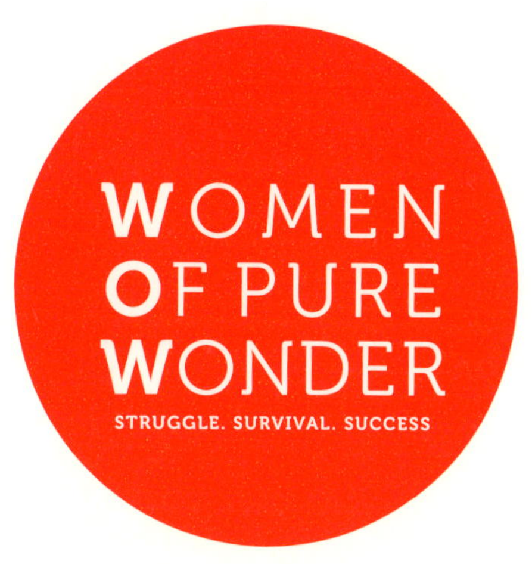

TEXT Ruchika Chanana & **Tanya** Luther
PHOTO EDITOR Ashima Narain

SHOWCASE
Roli Books

Women of Pure **Wonder**

'The idea of perfect womanhood
is perfect independence.'

Swami Vivekananda

Table of Contents

The **Leaders**

The **Healers**

Women of Renown

Shyam Benegal

Filmmaker, Former Member of Parliament

Women through the auteur's lens

At the stroke of the midnight hour, August 15, 1947, India attained freedom. But did the reality really change for women in India as well? Did they also attain freedom? We all know the answer to that one. The inequality between women and men is widely apparent – on the street, in offices, and even at home. It is hard to fathom the level of distress that civilized society experiences when regressive practices in the name of culture and customs still prevail.

Women, if given equal opportunities, can play a vital role in putting the country on the road to progress. Society loses a lot when women are kept in bondage – be it social, economic, or religious.

Sadly, the reality of today is not very different from yesterday – when having what it took wasn't good enough! Yet, some chose not to give up! Freedom comes at a price and some women – Smita Patil, Shabana Azmi, Neena Gupta, Ila Arun, and Rajeshwari Sachdev – were willing to walk that extra mile to be able to live life on their own terms. In spite of putting the same amount of time and effort into their work, they weren't even paid half of what their male counterparts received. They had to make an extra effort to be heard, to be seen, and to be taken seriously. Was it an easy journey? No. But was it worth it? Yes, maybe that is why they never gave up. What we need today is aspirational leadership and biographies of women who have done it before. We need to celebrate survivors, those who beat the odds and reached the top. That is what this book is all about.

One look around and it's not difficult to spot the unequal relationship that exists between men and women on the basis of social, economic, and religious parameters. Men have over the years put women in the reactive space, instead of the active space, so they are expected to react and not act. But it's really up to a woman to make that call. Acceptance can be a curse. My film *Bhumika*, dealt with this subject. When my protagonist realizes she can't depend on men and the only way she can empower herself is by being alone, she makes that choice. It's not easy, but it has to be done. Women not only earn, but run the house, give birth to a new life, nurture it, guide it; men can't do that. Yet, some call women the weaker sex!

I've always believed that empowerment should start at the bottom of the pyramid and a lot of work is being done at the grass-root level in various states. Such work, and the stories of such workers need to be shared, to be talked about and to be used as a role model. While working on my film *Manthan*, which concerned itself with the white revolution in Gujarat, I was amazed to see the participation of women in the panchayat, and the significant contributions they made towards the development of the state. Such stories need to be told, and then re-told. I am happy to say that this book celebrates the achievements of various women who work at this level.

Even today, the notion of 'equality' is not easy for society to accept. The need of the hour is self-empowerment as there is a lot at stake. Time has come for women to take what's rightfully theirs – the freedom to be.

Introduction

For every societal violence and manner of oppression that women are subjected to, there are diamonds in the rough who emerge kicking and screaming against the injustice. These rough jewels surface from time to time, and once hewn, not only do they shine bright and defy their circumstances, but they shine their light on other people and help them grow.

They constitute the people who wish for a unitary victory, not a solitary one; and a genius notion which only few and truly talented individuals are remembered in history books for.

This book stands for the power that 60 women have found within themselves. Their actions, which come from a determination to change their circumstances, are a force to reckon with. They have gone beyond their means to improve the future for themselves and the people around them, risking their financial and social status.

The world we glance at in the following pages is precious and aspirational. On perusing the pages of this book, there are brave and uplifting accounts to be read, that of a mother who became the first in her community to open a bank account so that she could keep her kids in school, the story about the waste picker who has a thing or two to say about self-respect, the journey of a polio survivor who from struggling to climb stairs went on to become an empowered entrepreneur, the acid attack victim who went on to define triumph, a battered housewife who defied regressive social norms, B-school graduates who chose social service over money, and many other driven women who have gone about fearlessly rejecting backward social practices like purdah, caste, the *devdasi* system, and child marriage traditions.

Today, society requires an especially concentrated effort from as many individuals, organizations, and factors possible to create an environment which imparts an equal status to women in family, society, and country. This is the sole motive of various programmes that are currently underway, and which are actively encouraging women empowerment.

This book is one such effort to salute the extraordinary achievements of India's warrior women and unsung heroines. For in a world such as ours, and in a place such as India, this is the sign of the humanity we need. The women here are a picture of success in an unequal world, shining bright like beacons of hope to other women, and a victory for them is a promise of a better future for the rest of us.

The **Entrepreneurs**

‘Strive constantly to serve
the welfare of the world;
by devotion to selfless work,
one attains the supreme goal of life.
Do your work with the welfare
of others always in mind.’

Lord Krishna, The Bhagwad Gita

Anita Kumbhar

Moulding dreams

Potter

In India, the caste you are born into often decides your profession. It is remarkably difficult to break away from that construct. The son of a priest must also be a priest, the daughter of a sweeper must resign herself for a life with the broom. In Anita Kumbhar's case, she imbibed the skill of pottery while growing up in a family of potters, and subsequently marrying into another one at a very young age. Anita, 35, tried to break away from the profession, but ultimately succumbed to the financial stability that it offered.

Not one to be beaten down, Anita, a native of Gondvale in Maharashtra, who had studied till grade ten found her own path within the confines of the pottery business. She created innovative designs and marketing techniques to create a product different from the usual *matkas* (mud pots for collecting and storing water) and *chulhas* (cooking stoves) that were traditionally made by potters, and were often seasonal.

'My mother-in-law used to make some small idols and figures as a hobby. I decided to see if other people would be interested in them, especially for festivals.' So she took a loan from a local rural bank, and started making an assortment of unique clay products in large numbers. Anita's strategy was brilliant.

Her products were customized for the various Indian festivals. And since there are so many festivals to be celebrated in India, her business flourished nearly all year round. She made idols of Ganeshas for Ganesh Chaturthi. Her tiny mud bullocks were a great hit at the livestock festival, Bendur. She even fashioned little soldiers, which could be given to children as Diwali gifts.

As her business grew, Anita decided she needed to enhance her skill set. She started going to MBA classes planned by the rural bank, learning to manage her earnings, carefully planning her income and expenditures. She began taking loans periodically in order to expand her business. She set up stalls at fairs, establishing a roaring trade, sometimes making up to 2,000 rupees a day.

Anita takes her responsibilities as a mother very seriously. 'My son is in grade four, and my elder daughter is in grade eight. They have big and beautiful dreams. My son wants to do engineering. I don't know if I will be able to save enough money to make their dreams come true. But what I do know is that I will give them the freedom to choose what they want to be in life, and not be bound by their caste. This is the reason why I work so hard.'

Nandini Lohar

Frame and fortune

Frame Maker and Doting Mother

The slight, sari clad woman hesitates at the door. Inside, the bank is bustling. People are on the phone, talking to each other, or just busy at their desks. Gathering herself, she woman walks in. The person at the counter smiles at her. She visibly relaxes, and her words come out in rush, 'I want a loan. Can you give me a loan?'

Later, the same woman, Nandini Lohar, 30, would laugh at that timid version of herself. 'I didn't know if they would treat me with dignity, or question my coming. I wasn't just nervous about whether they would say yes or no to my loan, I was also afraid that they would insult me. Nandini was the first person in her family to ever step into a bank.

She got her loan, and together with her husband, they invested in their business of making metal frames. After receiving the loan, they specialised in making metal frames for posters of Gondavle Karmaraj, the local deity of Gondavle, a temple town where they live. They sell these frames to the pilgrims who visit the deity every year.

Working with metal is Nandini's traditional profession – she belongs to a low caste of blacksmiths who usually live hand-to-mouth, working hard to make metal fences or sharpening farm equipment piecemeal, and squandering a large amount of what they earn on alcohol.

There is no impetus towards education. In such a scenario, Nandini and her husband stand out for their vision and entrepreneurial foresight. They live in a small hut and work from the same space. Nandini ventures out to the big city nearby to buy raw materials like wood, glass, plywood, glass-cutting instruments and posters. Her husband operates the plywood cutting machine. They then fashion the materials into frames.

Their profits are not very high, merely 2 rupees per piece when they sell wholesale. Recently, with the help of their latest loan, they have set up a stall so they can directly sell to the pilgrims, and that fetches them a higher profit. Still, they are better off than the rest of their people, some of whom have more or less ostracized them for being different.

Nandini doesn't care. She has repaid four loans to the bank. Her children go to school and she wants to keep them there. Some people in her community support her. She has savings, a concept unheard of among her people. The stability of their lives is a source of joy for her. She has even copyrighted her unique poster design and marketed it beautifully, helping her to corner the market.

And although she has the occasional sleepless night because she has had unforeseen expenditures and cannot repay her loans or buy raw materials, she manages to land on her feet every time. She borrows from friends or gets a temporary waiver from the bank. She knows every entrepreneur faces such challenges. She has practical knowledge about business: only through investing in infrastructure and building capacity can she expand her operation.

She has impressive plans for her children. 'I want to send my daughter to a vocational training college. My son wants to join the police, so I will help with that.' In 2010, Nandini was declared a 'Finalist' of the CII-Bharti Woman Exemplar Award.

Kiran Mazumdar Shaw

Pioneering new technology

Chairperson and MD, Biocon Limited

When I started Biocon in the garage of my rented house in Bangalore in 1978, the obstacles that I needed to navigate were manifold. In the seventies, entrepreneurship itself was an unusual 'career' choice for women. Moreover, my relative lack of experience in the nascent field of biotechnology, along with my gender and my youth were all perceived as huge handicaps. No bank wanted to lend to me, no professional wanted to work for me, and it was a challenge to set up a business because women had no credibility in the business world.

But overcoming each obstacle spurred me on towards success. I learnt to take on challenges one step at a time, and this helped boost my confidence. In due course of time, I was able to hold my own in a predominantly male bastion.

From a very frugal beginning, I slowly built Biocon up into a sizable enterprise through the team effort of many young scientists, engineers, and people who were as excited about creating a biotechnology business as I was. Today, Biocon is a cutting-edge biotechnology company valued at over a billion dollars. However, it took decades of hard work and unflinching commitment to create this value. We were underpaid and financially challenged, but we persevered with a sense of determination, battling all odds because of the excitement of our journey.

For both men and women, it is important to have their family's support and cooperation to succeed in their career. For women especially, balancing home and work life may become difficult without adequate support from the family. Even at the start of my entrepreneurial journey, I received the unstinted support of my family and friends, who encouraged me in my new endeavour and showed full faith in my entrepreneurial abilities. While it is true that I was single when I built Biocon, the real growth came about when I got married. My husband has played a vital role in our success.

Over the years, I have been felicitated on several occasions, which I believe is recognition of the value we have built for Brand Biocon. From one of the youngest woman recipients of Padma Shri in 1989, to Padma Bhushan in 2005. From Ernst & Young's Best Entrepreneur Award in 2002, to the *Economic Times* Businesswoman of the Year in 2004, to *Time*'s Top 100-most influential people in the world in 2010 – I have come a long way, and am humbled by every new recognition that I receive.

In my opinion, being a woman provides us with special attributes such as compassion, sensitivity, multi-tasking and above all, resilience to face and overcome challenges.

Success is about pursuing a vision with a sense of purpose and a spirit of challenge. It is led by not only 'doing different things' but also 'doing things differently'. My message to all enterprising women is that you must 'dare to dream'. Don't let the fear of failure come between you and your success. Remember, failure is temporary while giving up is permanent, so you should never give up but learn from your failures and set out to shape your dreams into reality.

YOU ARE A HERO
D for DASRA
46% of girls in India are child brides
educategirls.in

Neera Nundy

Living the dream

Partner and Co-founder, Dasra

Dasra means 'enlightened giving'. Neera Nundy and her husband Deval Sanghavi named their organization Dasra because their idea of doing good went beyond 'charity'. Bringing together philanthropists and social entrepreneurs to create an environment conducive to giving, Dasra is a unique idea. It is a model which if replicated, could transform the social sector in India.

It is interesting to note how a Canadian citizen, working as an analyst at Morgan Stanley in New York, ended up helping NGOs in India. Neera explains how the venture in philanthropy came about. 'My husband moved here and started Dasra. I finished business school and joined him two years later. We had been advising investors and valuing companies for so long. We wanted to apply the same principles to the social sector, and take the privilege of having been to business school and use that to help others.'

In the beginning, using their own money earned from occasional consulting jobs, Neera and Deval started seeding early-stage organizations. These included Magic Bus and Akshaya Patra (both NGOs are sector leaders now). They worked from home with a tiny staff. 'We've been around for 14 years, but it is only in the last few that we decided to scale ourselves up, and moved our intervention to professionalize the life cycle of the organization. We realized we wanted it to be more than a small, beautiful thing.'

Neera and her team, now 60-people strong, have created an innovative and highly effective education programme for social entrepreneurs called, Dasra Social-Impact. The idea was that even if a few of the 3.3 million non-profit organizations in India could learn how to use 'knowledge, funding opportunities, and people' to make their work more strategic, their impact and benefits would grow exponentially. Each year, 50 organizations graduate from the programme, some of these include Embrace, Industree and Lend-a-Hand. Another highly successful 'graduate' is Educate Girls, which is now flourishing in 4500 schools. Dasra helps such initiatives by establishing a methodology which strengthens their project management and addresses everything from salaries and HR, to finance and management.

Dasra's other point of focus is developing local philanthropy. The Indian Philanthropy Forum and Giving Circle have brought together a community given to discussing and implementing strategic philanthropy. These projects have streamlined over 15 million dollars in funds for social entrepreneurs.

Neera is proud of the impact Dasra has been able to have. 'We are inspired by the leaders of the social organizations, by philanthropists, and also by our own team. People motivate us. Managing growth is tough, as is keeping the cultural values of the organization intact, authentic, and relevant. Funding is a challenge too. We feel lucky to have the support and flexibility that we do. This is what keeps us going.' In the future, she envisions many Dasras all over India, modelled on this one.

Neera has three little boys, so she finds the balancing act quite stressful, but is very realistic when she says, 'Whose life isn't difficult?'

Vanita Pise

Empowering others

Manufacturer of Biodegradable Wares

Some people are born entrepreneurs. If you are born with talent but don't have the advantages of education and financial stability, it would be easy to miss out, or be missed out. However, if you are Vanita Pise, you create your own advantages.

Vanita, from Mhaswad in Maharashtra, dropped out of school in grade nine. She married into a rich family, had three children and then watched her world crumble as her husband's poultry business failed. This was in 1997. The family was broke, and in debt. Vanita took the reins. She tried many avenues: daily wage labour in other's fields; buffalo rearing and milk supplying (by taking a loan from a women's co-operative bank). Her husband and her in-laws didn't like her working outside the home, but Vanita persisted, struggling to keep home and hearth together.

Then one day, she came across the Self Help Group (SHG) movement. Suddenly, her outlook broadened, and her entrepreneurial skills had a chance to emerge. Her life, and that of her family, changed dramatically.

Vanita, 40, started producing paper cups, which are used for *prasad* or prayer offerings at temples. 'I saw an advertisement in the paper inviting people to make these cups, and I thought it was a good idea. The cups don't need much water, which we have a shortage of. They don't spoil easily, and they are biodegradable.'

In 2004, she decided to deepen her engagement with the business, and took a loan of 15,000 rupees. 'We have a local, socially-driven women's cooperative bank. This is good for us because they don't ask for too many documents; and because they know and trust me, it is easier to get a loan. And they also help with marketing,' she explains.

With this loan, she bought raw material, and a machine to increase the output of the paper cups. Vanita started churning out 5,000 cups a day. Her keen business acumen showed her the next step; she became a dealer for the machines, and facilitated 17 other women in starting their own ventures.

Today, Vanita's business and her income have grown exponentially. 'I now have machines for making cups, for crushing wheat, and also a new one for making the big *thalis* (plates) people use at weddings. My total investment in these is 2 lakhs.' She also employs six women.

Her success did not go unnoticed. In 2006, she received national recognition as one of the winners of the CII-Bharti Woman Exemplar Award from the Prime Minister of India. This honour is given annually to 'grass-root, poor, under-privileged community level women who have excelled in their contribution to the development process. The main duty of the person who receives the award is to empower others.'

By helping her sisters initiate income-generating activities, and by making sure her children are educated to the highest levels (especially her two daughters), Vanita has provided inspiration, training and guidance to so many people: this is empowerment of the best kind.

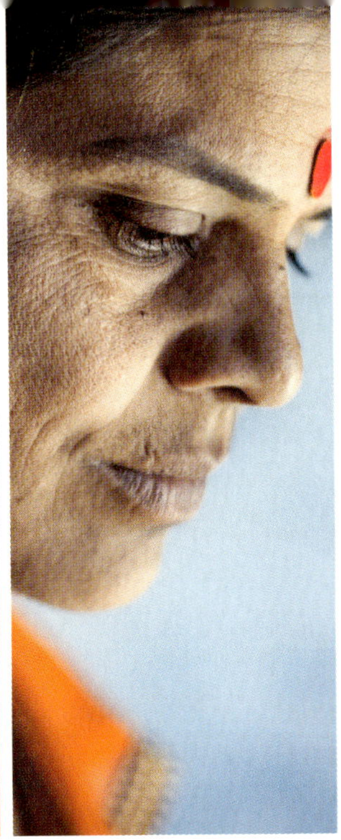

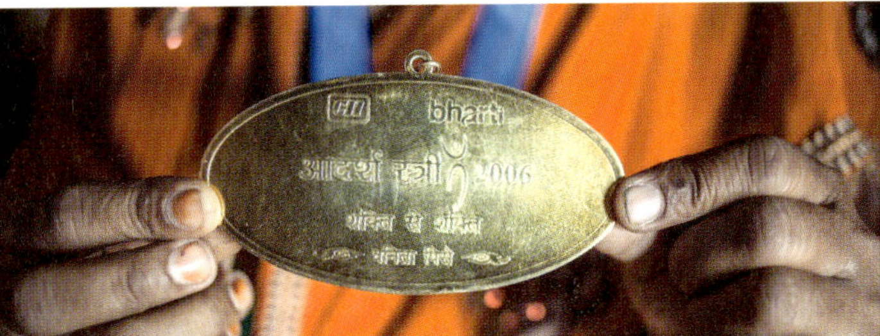
CII
bharti
आदर्श स्त्री 2006

Priti Paul

Empowered by her father's faith

Director Apeejay Group and Creator, Oxford Bookstore

I was born in Calcutta into a large, loving, and supportive family. I had a happy, simple childhood, filled with books. When I turned 18, we moved to Delhi. The same summer, I travelled to Boston to join Massachusetts Institute of Technology, where I studied architecture and economics. Education was very important in our family, especially to my mother who was well-educated and came from a cultured, though simple background. My mother was the first female employee American Express hired in India.

There were two dramatic turning points in my life – when my brother Anand was killed in a car accident, and when my father was assassinated by United Liberation Front of Assam (ULFA) terrorists in the spring of 1990, the same year I graduated. My mother held everything together and she supported us kids in all our endeavours, including taking on the businesses, which at that time had over 50,000 employees.

I moved to London to take care of Apeejay Shipping and began to manage a dynamic and evolving bulk-carrier business, while at the same time continuing my studies. I closed my first deal at a shipyard in Poland when I was 21, without knowing the language, and surrounded by men. It was a multi-million dollar deal, and I managed it because of my education, where I had competed with the best students at the best universities in the world. This instilled in me a sense of purpose and confidence. The fact that I grew up in a business family also helped. But the biggest factor was my survival instinct. I said to myself: 'Have courage, make the decision...' A few years later, I went to Harvard to do another master's in architecture.

Being a woman has been an asset to me. My father always said that he expected nothing less of me than he would from a son. That was an amazing thing for him to say in the 80's, and it gave me tremendous self-confidence. He gave us projects and businesses to run from a young age, so that we could learn to be accountable.

I now handle the real estate section of our company in India. I also manage the Oxford Bookstores. The first bookstore was the iconic one in Calcutta, which had been around for over 90 years. It was part of the social, emotional, and cultural fabric of the city, as well of my life. So when I was 23, I thought of re-inventing the store and the space, and maybe taking it to other cities. World Bank expressed an interest in this project, but I went ahead on my own

I met my husband Jaouad Kadiri a decade ago while on holiday in Marrakech. I now live between Marrakech, New Delhi, and London. I feel that a supportive spouse helps the careers of both, husband and wife.

I am always asked how I maintain a balance between work and my personal life. I hate this question. There is no balance – it tips in different directions at different times. When my boys Jad, Kais, and Jai were young, my motherhood took precedence. Being a mother is an all-consuming thing, but I also believe in putting passion and deep commitment into my work. To me, there is no choosing between the personal and professional – they are linked. I think of investing time in my children as being akin to investing in the future of my business.

Empowerment means having choices, and also the ability to exercise those choices. The reason behind the presence of said choices might be many – intelligence, talent, fame, support, money, ambition, luck.... Or perhaps a combination of these. For me, education and my father's faith in me are what empower me the most.

I am a very goal-oriented person and have been like that since I was a little girl. What I have tried to learn over the years is that the goals are always important, but it's also important to enjoy the journey and be transformed by it.

Rekha

A recycled life

Waste Manager, Kissan Haat and Artemis Hospital

Seldom do we give a thought to the hands that collect waste from our homes, restaurants, offices, schools, and streets. The waste-pickers of any city are crucial components of the recycling loop and vital intermediaries in the informal economy. They salvage reusable materials and direct recyclable ones to factories to earn a livelihood.

Yet, they are shunned by the community at large and harassed by the authorities. They lead lamentable lives and have heartrending stories to tell.

Rekha, 35, a migrant from Bihar, was widowed at the age of 20. 'My husband had barely spent time with our three-month-old baby when he lost his life in an accident. My in-laws supported me for a while but it was difficult for them to support my son and me beyond a point.

We were so poor that we often went hungry for several days,' says Rekha. Family members advised her to migrate to Delhi to look for work. 'It was an emotionally difficult decision to leave my village and head to *pardes* (foreign land).'

In 1998, Rekha moved to the Capital to live with her brother for a few weeks before she settled down in a slum on her own. 'My brother suggested I pick waste to earn money so I began scavenging through trash for plastic. It was a start and I could feed my son,' she says. But there were troubles along the way. 'Picking up trash from the city's dumps is hazardous work. One has to avoid getting injured by falling items, or being hit by moving vehicles while scrambling to get to the recyclable materials being dumped. Then there were frequent arguments between workers and sweepers about territory and claims to materials of value. The local police exploited the fact that I had no *pehchaan patra* (identification) and because of this, I had to bribe them every week. Most people looked at me with suspicion and contempt, calling scavenging a dirty job.'

Along the way Rekha married a man from the same profession. She worked in the day and her husband worked at night. Their pooled resources took care of their needs. In 2011, Rekha became acquainted with Chintan, an environmental and research action group, and Safai Sena, a registered group of waste pickers. Trained by both groups she began working at Kisaan Haat, a crafts bazaar in Delhi in 2012.

Rekha is now a supervisor and manages waste at the bazaar and for Artemis Hospital. She leads a team of 12 women. 'Chintan showed me how to cope with the tribulations of work and family life and provided me with opportunities to meet people from around the world. I wear a uniform at work and am a respected member of society. People look up to me. I want to enable my team members so they too can fend for themselves in a dignified manner. I am an empowered woman and I refuse to bribe policemen anymore,' she says with gratitude.

Rekha says that she now 'walks like a man', intrepid and dauntless.

CORNPUFF

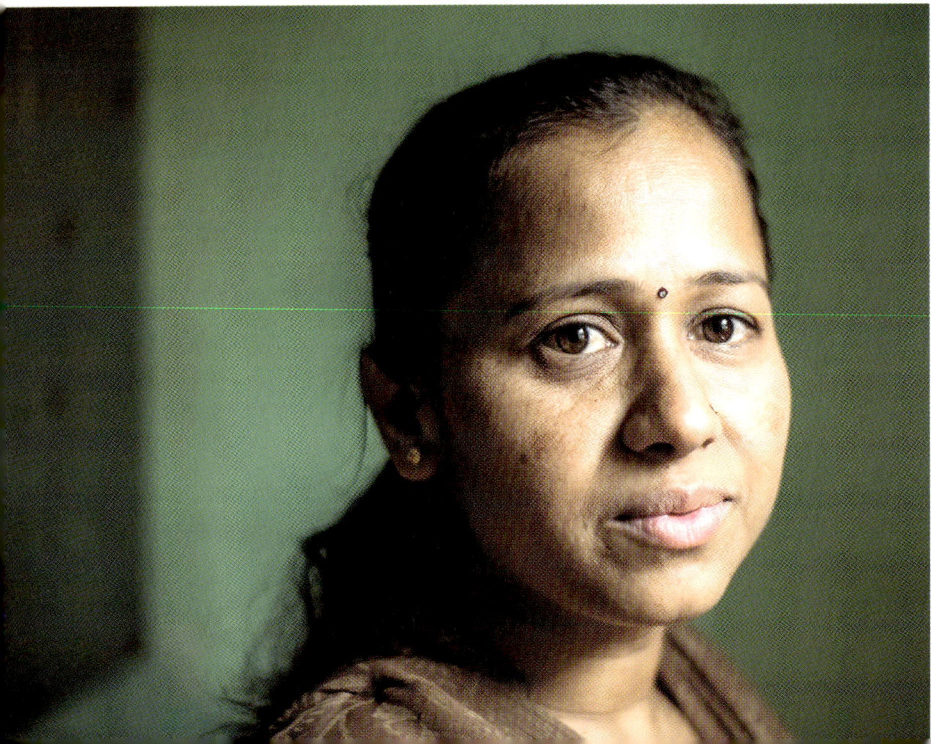

स्वामी समर्थ
जनरल स्टोअर्स
सिमरन लेडीज वेअर

Shobha Raut

Self abled

Stay-at-home Entrepreneur

Shobha Raut, 33, appears handicapped only when she uses her crutches to walk. For all practical purposes, she is a woman who stands tall on her own feet.

Polio-stricken when she was just 10 months old, Shobha grew up with hardships in her village, Mhaswad in the Satara district of Maharashtra. However, even as a child, Shobha was determined to excel. She travelled to a neighbouring town by bus to get to school. She earned her graduate degree in commerce and set out to live a life of dignity on her own terms.

Shobha interviewed for jobs but on her way to the first one, she slipped on the staircase leading to the office. When she finally found a job, she fell yet again on her way to work and broke her arm. 'There are no handicap-friendly facilities where I live and it continues to be difficult to get around,' she says.

Finally, she set up a grocery shop at home in the hope that she would gain economic independence and also support her younger brother's education. 'I tried twice over in five years to make a success of the venture but it failed both times. I began by purchasing a kilo each of various groceries and even scaled it to five kilos. Then things got difficult as I had to walk 30 minutes to and fro to procure items,' says Shobha.

Disheartened but not defeated, Shobha mustered up the courage to seek a bank loan. 'I was a regular customer at the bank and was aware of the various loan schemes. I applied for a loan at 11 am and walked out of the bank at 3 pm the same day with 15,000 rupees in hand. I also got advice from the bank to set up a business selling sari blouses.' She took the advice and found that she was spared of the commute every day as suppliers were happy to deliver the items to her.

Business picked up and Shobha repaid her loan ahead of time. She took a second loan the following year to stock stationery items. 'It's a long workday from 6 am to 10 pm, all seven days of the week. My mother helps as much as she can and I feel happy that I have been able to fulfil my responsibilities,' says Shobha. 'My brother is now a postgraduate student in computer software studies. I have borrowed 2 lakh rupees from the bank for the purpose of expanding my business and house repairs.'

In 2010, Shobha did the unthinkable. She undertook a 100 km *padyatra*, a foot pilgrimage, to a temple in Satara district to pay reverence to her god. She, however, thinks nothing of the distance she covered on crutches but only that her renewed faith keeps her going.

This young, dynamic woman looks towards the future with hope and conviction. 'I have no desire to get married. I am self-reliant and want to care for my aging parents,' she says. 'As for my business, I want it to grow and I will expand my operations but only after I assess my risks.'

Shobha now mentors other women entrepreneurs. Her veritable triumph over her disability makes her an empowered woman.

Trishala Dangare

Energizing lives

Biomass Stove Marketer

In 1993, the Latur district in Maharashtra was the epicentre of a devastating earthquake, which left thousands of people homeless and just as many children orphaned. Seismologists explain the release of stored potential energy from rocks as a phenomenon that occurs after an earthquake. Metaphorically speaking, Trishala Dangare of Latur exemplifies this phenomenon.

Wed into a joint family, Trishala, all of 35, found that her household duties superseded and sidelined her education and master's degree in commerce. Even so, she was driven by the conviction, 'Everything that is new should be mine.' Out on a shopping trip in a rural area of Latur, Trishala stopped to look at an unusual cooking stove. She tracked down the manufacturer and subsequently the distributor Swayam Shikshan Prayog (SSP).

The *Oorja* stove was a revelation for Trishala. The stove is a biomass-based cooking solution, fired by fuel pellets made from agricultural waste, a brilliant alternative to firewood and its toxic fumes. Trishala's mind lit up with the opportunities it could offer to women in rural areas. Initially, her family discouraged her business proposition but eventually her husband supported her decision to begin marketing the stoves. Given her fledgling start-up enterprise, Trishala spawned her business plan with a door-knocking approach, making herself in-charge of her business. However, one week and a 100 households later, she had managed just one sale. This was the beginning of her first business relationship with a customer.

Soon, word spread and the customer shared the experience with others, raving about saving time, money, and energy by using the stove. The demand for the stoves grew manifold and Trishala expanded the width of her product mix to solar lights, water purifiers, fuel pellets, and more. She carved a niche for herself and held a monopoly in the market as the only agency to sell eco-friendly products in the rural areas of Maharashtra. Yet, there were challenges aplenty: low profit margins, low working capital, and a need for more after-sales services. Trishala signed up for a course in entrepreneurship at Sakhi Sandhi Business School and learned critical skills in sales and marketing techniques. She has empowered herself further by taking a loan from Rang De, a micro-lending non-profit outfit in an effort to diversify her business.

'I want to increase sales and diversify, but I have constraints of manpower and finances. If I could afford a two-wheeler I would learn to ride it and cover areas beyond the 12 to 15 kms I normally reach by bus or auto. I am dependent on training personnel from SSP to accompany me and given their busy schedules, I have to sometimes forego a village visit. I need more training for myself to be independent,' she says.

A mother of three teenage children, Trishala wants to tackle her competition by introducing new products and of a varied price range. Her 18-year-old son helps to repair the *Oorja* stoves. 'He is self-taught and is already learning the ropes of the business,' she remarks proudly. 'It's not all business though,' she says. 'I love to cook new recipes for my family.' This entrepreneur and homemaker keeps it all together through meditation. 'I wake up at five in the morning and meditate. It keeps me calm and gives me peace of mind.' While Trishala continues to spread awareness amongst rural women, there is one thing to be said about her, it's all about the energy!

Shahnaz Husain

Beauty, heart, and soul

Chairperson and MD, Shahnaz Husain Group of Companies

I never planned it this way. My life was on a very different course. I belong to a traditional family. I was engaged at 14 and married by 15. By the time I was 16, I had become a mother. Life seemed perfect, but I was bored with the drudgery of an endless routine. I always wanted to be a person who made a difference. I was interested in beauty and in making others beautiful. So, I decided to choose beauty as a career. My husband was posted in Tehran. I started writing articles for the *Iran Tribune* and paid my way to the best beauty schools like Helena Rubinstein (London), Christine Valmy (New York), Swarzkopf (Germany), Lancome (Paris), and Lean (Copenhagen). So, despite lacking a university education, I managed to earn enough to get the best training in cosmetology and cosmetic therapy.

While training in London, I came across the damage caused by chemical treatments. It changed the course of my career. I wanted to find a safe alternative to the chemical treatments, and knew that I must have my own enterprise in order to translate my ideas to reality. So, I opened my first herbal salon in the verandah of my own home after borrowing 35,000 rupees from my father. I started making my own formulations, using plant products and natural ingredients. I made the products at night, filled them in jars, wrote and labeled them by hand.

Having pioneered the concept of 'herbal care and cure', the first hurdle was to make people aware of herbal healing and dangers of chemicals. Four decades ago, communication was not what it is today. I started contributing articles to newspapers in which I provided home remedies. In the minds of the readers, this reinforced my philosophy that 'nature is the best cosmetologist'. It became an integral part of the brand image of my products.

I fought a lone battle again, when I entered the international market during the Festival of India in 1980. I was given a counter at Selfridges, the famous London store, competing with the biggest brand names. In the face of fierce competition, I stood my ground and promoted the image of 'India and Ayurveda'. To stand up alone and sell India's ancient civilization in a jar was not easy. To everyone's surprise, we sold out our consignment in three days, breaking the store's cosmetic sales records. The next day there was a headline in a London daily, 'Herbal Hell Breaks Loose in Selfridges!' Today, Shahnaz is the only Indian herbal beauty brand sold at Selfridges.

I believe that a career, financial independence, and self-reliance are extremely important for women's empowerment. I adopted a franchise-based enterprise, providing opportunities to Indian housewives to open salons in their own homes. Thus they can have a career yet be close at hand to take care of their home and family. I am also committed to providing free beauty courses to physically challenged girls.

As a proud Indian, I have spoken from every rostrum on Ayurveda. I recently lectured at Massachusetts Institute of Technology, USA and have also spoken at Harvard Business School, Oxford University and London School of Economics. Recently, I was invited to speak at the House of Lords and House of Commons, and walked the red carpet at the Cannes Film Festival 2013. I have received several prestigious awards like the World's Greatest Woman Entrepreneur from the New York based *Success* magazine, as well as the Award for Innovation by the British Parliament, and the Padma Shri.

Deterrents come up in life, but I take them on like challenges with my desire to excel, my relentless determination to succeed and sheer hard work. To every woman who wants to become an entrepreneur, I would say that it is an advantage to acquire professional training in your field. Keep learning. The sky is the limit. Never give up. If you never give up, you cannot fail. You may start small but always think big. You have to know that nothing is beyond you ... nothing is impossible. You can be whatever you will yourself to be. You can create your own destiny. Dare to dream, then do everything within your power to make your dream come true.

Vijaya Patsala

Buzzing businesswoman

Beekeeping Promoter and Trainer

It is feared that if bee colonies in the wild continue to perish, we may have an empty dinner plate on our table. It is said that the honeybee is more honoured than other animals, not because she labours, but because she labours for others. One woman is on a mission to help these precious pollinators thrive so they may create a healthy eco-system for us.

Vijaya Patsala, 47, did not receive an education in beekeeping or the business of it. She has a bachelor's in International Relations and Women's Studies from Mount Holyoke College, USA and a master's in Regional Planning from the Massachusetts Institute of Technology, USA. 'In the last six years, I have learned from my venture all that I would have at a business school,' she says.

In 1994, Vijaya volunteered with relief efforts in the earthquake-stricken Latur, Maharashtra. She noticed that the community interacted, traded and exchanged news under the shade of mango trees in the area. The observation stayed with her, and even before she conceived a business enterprise to launch, she had a name for it: Under the Mango Tree (UTMT). 'There was no catalytic moment to the mission of UTMT but I knew I wanted to address farmers' productivity. Over time, I realized that no one was working towards facilitating natural pollination. Bees pollinate four to five of the foods we eat, like pulses, oil seeds, fruits, and vegetables. They can increase yield by 60 per cent,' she says. For two years, Vijaya studied market creation for gourmet honey, consumer tastes, beekeeping trends, and government policies. 'In 2007, there was a large knowledge gap amongst consumers about single origin honey and what made a good quality honey. In 2009 we charged to implement one idea – honey, pollination, and bees for poverty reduction.' UTMT set out with two objectives: to train farmers to add beekeeping on their farms to address livelihood diversification, agricultural productivity, and improved income, and to create direct, fair-trade and sustainable market access from farmers to consumers.' We began operations with a seed capital of 3 lakh rupees to procure honey from across the country and sell it at exhibitions and crafts stalls,' says Vijaya.

The idea was fraught with challenges. 'I had little operational expertise and it was extremely difficult to raise funds to scale up our operations. But I believed in the idea of doing something good. Along the way I met people who had enough faith in my vision to sign me a cheque,' she shares. Vijaya was determined to find a viable solution for markets that desired quality organic certified, all-natural products but had a limited and inconsistent chain of suppliers. And she did find a solution. Over six years, UTMT has trained more than 1,400 farmers in beekeeping and demonstrated a 50 per cent increase in crop yield. This has helped increase their income up to 12,000 rupees annually. The NGO has also provided 1,500 small beekeepers direct market access for their honey, thereby increasing their annual income by 25 per cent.

'We have proven ourselves and our products are now visible in gourmet spaces and niche markets in major cities,' says Vijaya. UTMT recently received a grant of $ 100,000 from India Development Marketplace funded by the World Bank. 'We are now financially viable and can look ahead. We have made a foray into Madhya Pradesh and aim to reach 10,000 farmers in the state.' Vijaya acknowledges the support from her husband. She wants to do the same for aspiring entrepreneurs. 'I want to motivate women and share my experience and journey thus far. It's not easy to balance family with work. Our society and immediate ecosystem is yet to evolve to bolster women's empowerment. It's always the woman who is expected to maintain that balance.'

Sheelu Singh **Rajput**

Rebel song

Aalha Performance Artist

The young girl sits with her chin in hand, watching the images flit about on the screen. The VHS tape emits a faint buzz, which combines with the slightly distorted audio of the recording. On the screen, a man, dressed as a warrior, brandishes a sword and sings in a loud, high-pitched voice. Every flourish of his sword or his tone makes the girl's eyes shine brighter, and she mouths the lyrics of the song. She wants to be just like him when she grows up.

Sheelu Singh Rajput, 18, is no ordinary village girl. Now grown up, she has made her childhood dream come true. She has become an Aalha singer. Generally a male bastion, Aalha is a folk music tradition of Uttar Pradesh in the Awadhi dialect in which singers describe and act out stories of the great kings, Aalha and Udal, and their valourous deeds. Sheelu has broken the convention and leapt into the fray, despite being a girl. She and her contemporaries have added more stories to the mix, including the tale of the brave Rani of Jhansi.

Always interested in music, Sheelu used to sing *bhajans* (hymns), but her favourite memories are of her father reading Alha stories to her. 'I always had a fascination for it and tried to recite them in my own way. Hearing the stories was nice, but then we saw some videos. I loved them, especially the swordplay! I thought if I became a performer, I could also wave a sword about. Then I saw a woman from Madhya Pradesh performing Aalha, and I decided this was what I wanted to do.' She performed for the first time at the Hanuman temple near her home. During her performance, she was spotted by Aalha Samrat Sri Lallu Bajpai, one of the most popular proponents of the form and someone who Sheelu had watched videos of growing up. Seeing her talent, he asked her to join his group, and trained her in the correct techniques. 'He taught me every thing I know. Sadly, he died recently. But he told me to continue singing, so that people can always remember this tradition of ours.'

Her parents are supportive and proud of her achievements as a singer and as a woman. 'They feel I have brought honour to our family's name,' she says. Do they not worry about her getting married? 'There is no pressure on me, I can marry when I want to.' Sheelu is pursuing her second year of bachelor's. 'My studies are important too. When I have exams, I cut down on my performances.'

Confident and assured, Sheelu knows what she wants. She would like to sing for as long as she can, because it is her passion – but also because it has done so much for her. 'How can I explain what Aalha means to me? It has given me knowledge and exposure to the world, of what is outside my village. And I can earn money for my family and for my studies.'

Sheelu has performed on several stages, in Benaras, Bhopal, even in Delhi, sharing the limelight with film stars and local singers. She sings, she acts, she emotes– she explains that it is all about communicating something to the audience. 'This is our history. These old folk songs are getting lost. Kids today don't know anything about them. I want to bring to them traditions of the village and show the world how rich they are. I want to spread Aalha all over.'

Vijaylakshmi

Crediting success

Spice Shop Owner

Vijaylakshmi sits in her small shop, spices of different hues piled up in front of her and assorted packets of snacks hanging behind. Her head is covered with her sari *pallu* (head covered with the loose end of the sari). and she looks demure, restrained, and dependent. Looks, however, can be deceptive.

This entrepreneur started a retail business, put her four children through school and has now bought a house. Her shop continues to be her source of pride and income. Business is thriving, and she looks content. 'My husband does all the outside work, and I run the shop,' she says. But life is not all rosy for Vijaylakshmi. She also has to do housework and take care of her young children, besides her second job. This is the job that has changed her life.

Several years ago, members of a Self Help Group (SHG) called Shramik Bharti came to Jana village, where Vijaylakshmi lives with her family. They explained the idea of a co-operative savings scheme to the villagers. 'We didn't trust them at first,' says Vijaylakshmi, candidly. 'We started by putting in 10 rupees every month. The activists were patient, winning the trust of the people slowly through transparency of operations and by providing easy access to loans. 'Slowly it has come to a point where we are putting in 200 rupees per month!' This programme, also implemented in 100 other such villages, became the Boond Bachat Sangathan (or Saving Drop by Drop Group).

The savings helped women like Vijaylakshmi improve their lives considerably. Habituated into saving every month, the women no longer depended on unscrupulous moneylenders for emergencies. They did not live a hand-to-mouth existence anymore, and could pay their own medical bills as well. They could send their children to school, and still have money left over to invest in entrepreneurial schemes, income generation activities, or in a proper roof over their heads. 'I have taken many loans from the Sangathan over the years, more than 20 in fact, and paid them all back, usually at 1,000 rupees per month. The first loan was for 15,000 rupees, and now I have taken one for 40,000 rupees to build my house.'

The second aim of the SHG was for the community to understand their common issues, discuss them and take charge of finding solutions. The group members meet once a month to tackle issues like water and hygiene. 'We have managed to install water taps here, also some latrines in the village. This has made a lot of difference,' says Vijaylakshmi who is now an active member of the SHG. Training women in stitching or crafts has added to the self-sufficiency of the villagers. 'Women have to go out of their houses so they can learn more about the world outside, the village and the cities. We also need to get together and communicate with others about our problems, whether they are physical abuse or bad roads. This is how we will progress,' she says.

Like her SHG, there are around 15 other SHGs in the village, explains Vijaylakshmi. She attempts to bring more members into the fold of the credit and thrift groups by explaining the advantages to the others. 'We can do so much more, but people need to be motivated and get out of their homes. I have so many ideas, I can do so much – I just need support.'

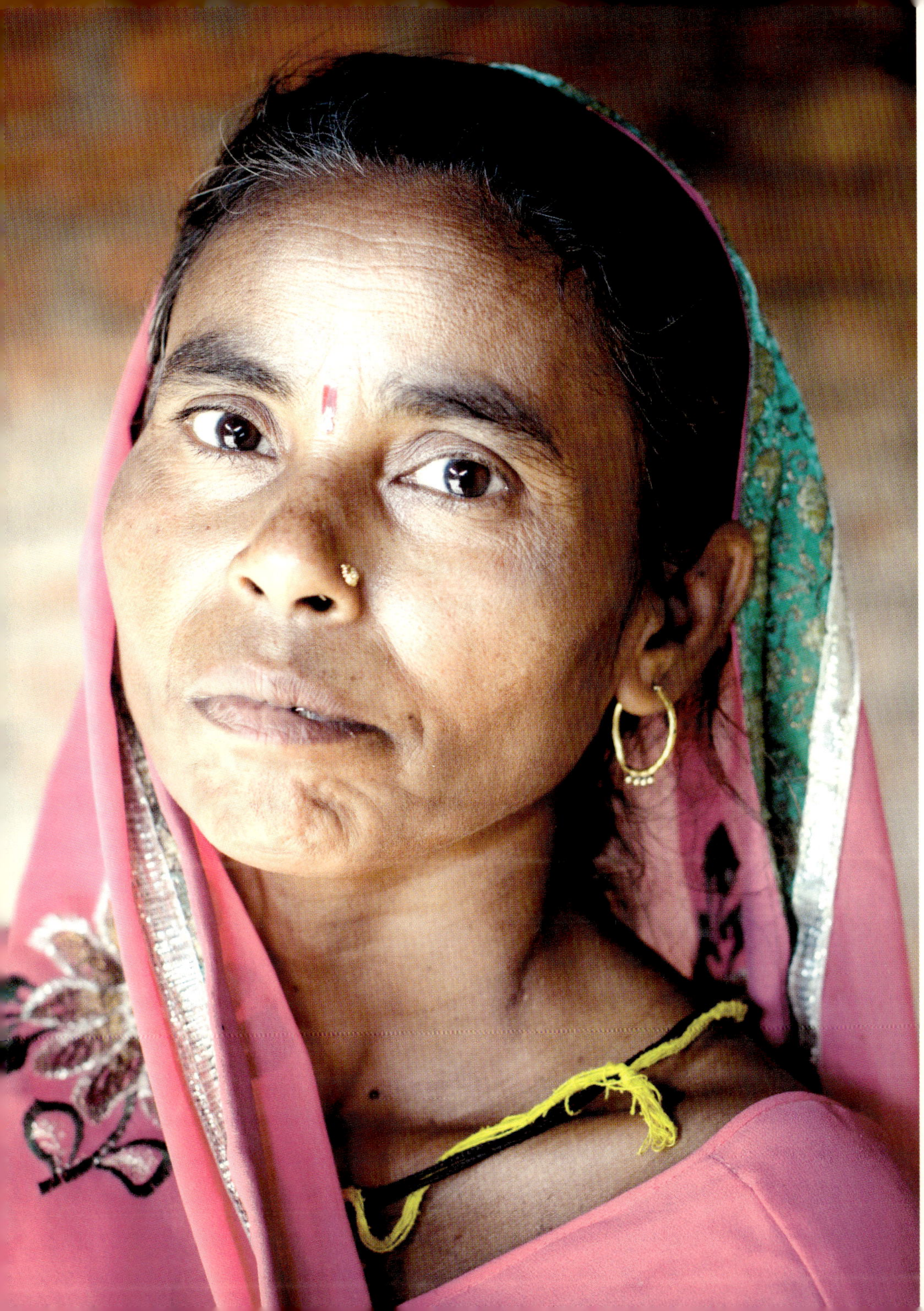

श्रमिक भारती
कानपुर
द्वारा
प्रोत्साहित
बूंद बचत संघ, कुलगाँव, कानपुर
स्वयं सहायता समूह
सदस्य पास बुक

Zarina Screwvala

Every step a discovery

Co-Founder UTV (Now Disney UTV) and Co-Founder and Managing Trustee, The Swades Foundation

Everything I have or have done in my life is a gift from other people and I am grateful to them all. I started life as a shy girl who was bullied at school, in Washington D.C. where my father was the Naval and Military Attaché. Sadly, I never told my parents who would have turned the school upside down! My parents are wonderful people, who gifted me and my lovely brother with the most important things in life – a loving family and a strong moral code. The home we lived in gave me an everlasting love for trees. Being shy, I preferred to spend my time either with my family or in the glorious cherry tree in the yard! In fact, when people would ask me what I wanted to do in life, I would reply in all seriousness, 'I want to climb trees'. And in a way, that's exactly what I have been doing all my life. And what a joy it has been!

We soon came back to Mumbai and I joined the J.B. Petit High School for Girls, where I met my future mentors and guides: our iconic principal Ms. Shirin Darasha, theatre personality Pearl Padamsee, and sculptor and artist Pilloo Poachkhanawala. These three dynamic women were at the top of their game, and they taught me – without ever saying it – that women can be anything they want to be. I suddenly lost all my shyness and became pretty much the person I am today.

Right through school and college, I would act and paint. These interests gave me confidence and an abiding love for beauty. But when it came to deciding what to do in life, I was as confused as many young people are today. By sheer luck, I joined Ronnie Screwvala when he was directing India's first independent production *Mashoor Mahal* as assistant director. And then, UTV was born with Ronnie at the helm. It has given me such fulfillment to co-create a vibrant, cutting edge company that believes passionately in creativity and content from its core. Initially, we were television-centric. We produced India's very first daily soap, *Shanti*, and the first game show *Snakes & Ladders*. In 2005, I decided that 19 years in TV was as good as it would get, thousands of shows for almost every broadcaster, loads of hits, some misses, awards; it was all great fun but it was time to move on. Ronnie calls this one of my many 'restless' phases. I planned to take a year long sabbatical and paint, but after ten days of my Vipassana meditation course, I was back at work (thanks to Ronnie) and the only person who was surprised was me!

Hungama TV was India's first local kids channel. I took it on six months after the launch when it was at 26 GRP's (Gross Rating Points). Cartoon Network was numero uno at approximately 200 GRP's. My team and I re-launched the channel and our innovations took it to the top spot in just 12 months. It felt great! We then got an outstanding offer from Disney to buy Hungama and decided to take it. Eventually, we sold UTV to Disney for an enterprise value of 1.4 billion USD. Though I was mildly heartbroken, it was then that Disney invested in UTV, and our relationship has since been a fabulous win-win.

I became essentially jobless and was moping around wondering what to do with myself and sat down one afternoon and created the entire concept that was to become the youth channel, UTV Bindass. Today, Bindass is also at the top spot, but gets a load of competition from decade-old global brands, but we (mostly) put them in their place! I love the fact that our Indian-born brands beat global giants!

Six months after the sale, and much to everyone's shock, I decided to leave my beloved UTV after 27 years to work with our Foundation full time. I felt the need to think about different challenges. I basically love people and I love problems, the bigger and more complex the problem is, the better! What could be more challenging than a new job? The single-minded aim of the Swades Foundation is rural empowerment, to transform the lives of one million people in rural India over the next five years and to lift them out of poverty, permanently through a super-intensive 360-degree model we have designed. The model encompasses community mobilization, water and sanitation, livelihood and agriculture, education, and health and nutrition.

I also paint occasionally, practice the wonderful technique of Vipassana meditation, and have joined an amazing philosophy class called New Acropolis. Please do try all three!

The **Teachers**

'Only one person in a million
becomes enlightened
without a teacher's help.'

Bodhidharma

Gulafsha Khan

Mentor. Guide. Leader

Teacher, Magic Bus

Not far from the historic city of the erstwhile Mughal rulers, Delhi, is the large settlement colony of Bhalswa. In stark contrast to the grandeur of the capital city, Bhalswa can best be described as Delhi's largest dumping ground. It is difficult to conceive that the shantytown is home to thousands of families who were evicted from slums in Delhi and resettled near a landfill site. It is even harder to believe that a young girl could rise like a phoenix from under the pervasive haze of the putrid and toxic methane gas.

Gulafsha Khan was a young girl when her family was forced to move to Bhalswa. 'We lived in a slum in Nizammudin in South Delhi with access to clean water and electricity. We were horrified when we got to Bhalswa. The area was a desolate jungle swarming with snakes. People were so despondent that they wanted to run away. When the settlers began digging the earth to stand their shelters, they found countless bones. It was a creepy place,' recalls Gulshafa. Her five siblings and parents struggled to make ends meet then and it is not very different now. Most of the community's population is well below the poverty line. Men and women work as daily wage workers at construction sites while some women find employment as maids in more affluent areas nearby.

Over time, the settlement degenerated into a slum while the peripheral area developed with the setting up of two primary schools and one secondary school. Gulafsha and her five siblings found their way to school while living in a one-room slum with their parents. In 2011, Gulafsha heard about the NGO Magic Bus from her friends. She went to meet its volunteers, Santosh and Mahadev, and learned that Magic Bus worked to drive change in the areas of education, health and hygiene and reproductive health. Gulafsha says, 'I signed up for the Community Youth Leader (CYL) programme. After my six-day training, I had to make a group of 25 kids and teach through play. I approached several parents to permit their children to join the activities in a nearby park. Many declined for safety reasons. I had to build their trust in me over time to prove to them that I was a responsible girl.' The volunteers at Magic Bus recognized Gulafsha's enthusiasm and extraordinary mentoring skills and awarded her CYL of the month. They consistently encouraged her to pursue her education while gently cajoling her parents to agree.

Subsequently, Gulafsha joined the Connect programme, a special programme which trained the Magic Bus CYLs in Functional English, computer literacy, and interview-readiness skills. 'The Connect Programme has helped me a lot. After completing the course, I feel confident. There's also a remarkable improvement in my verbal English,' said Gulafsha.

'It has not been easy for me to step out to work. My community has constantly taunted my parents for letting me work and in turn my parents have often pressured me to abandon social work. When I am with my group of children I feel like a child again. In the time that I spend with them, I forget my worries about the present and the future entirely.'

Gulafsha realized that her parents could not afford her college education so she began giving home tuitions to middle-school children. 'I now pay my college fee from my earnings,' says Gulafsha. 'I want to study further to qualify for a teacher's job.'

Gulafsha, 19, wants to live life on her own terms and she does today.

Magic bus
PREMIER LEAGUE

Magic bus

परमेश्वर का अनुग्रह
तुझ पर हुआ है
Milkman

Hasina Anand

Pursuing happiness

Programme Officer, Thane and Ray Road Shelter Homes

As a young girl Hasina Anand did not know of Nelson Mandela, let alone be acquainted with his truism, 'Education is the most powerful weapon which you can use to change the world.' Her birth and upbringing as a girl child in an orthodox Muslim family in Mumbai with five siblings was hardly conducive to nursing dreams of a grand future. While her brothers received preferential education in English medium schools, she and her sisters were sent to municipal schools. She was expected to accept the restrictions imposed on her and the opportunities granted to her brothers. She watched her mother live a life devoid of dignity and this raised a tiny voice in her head that made her want Mandela's powerful weapon: education. She began by changing her little world.

Hasina realized over time that she could bend her parents' conservative precepts when she articulated a desire for something. 'I was twelve years old when I asked for permission to wear a T-shirt. I was surprised when my parents yielded. So I continued to ask and eventually I was able to complete my high school education. I knew by then that I wanted to be a teacher. So I went on to become a trained Montessori teacher.'

These were big strides for Hasina. Armed with an education, Hasina joined the Community Outreach Programme (CORP) in 1983 as a crèche teacher in the disadvantaged locale of Dharavi. 'My father was extremely unhappy that I had picked up a job but then he visited the crèche. He watched me interact with little children and realized that I was passionate about and devoted to working for a social cause. His disapproval turned to appreciation and I have had his unconditional support since.' In three years, Hasina continued to hone her skills through opportunities provided by CORP. She received training in entrepreneurship, dug deep into the nuances of community development in Gujarat and completed a six month teacher training course in Sangli, Maharashtra. Her hunger for education drove her to earn a bachelor's degree. Hasina had set out on a journey and she prodded on to live her dream.

In 1986 Hasina was promoted to supervisor at CORP's Thane zone. She brought forward her rich experience and zeal to set up a *balwadi* (pre-school for low-income families) and crèche. This exceptionally driven woman is now a Programme Officer at the Thane and Ray Road centres and runs the shelter homes with a lot of conviction. 'Our Thane Centre comprises of three community centres in the slum areas of Kailash Nagar, Indira Nagar, and Boudha Vihar. We cater to *mahila mandals* (women's Self Help Groups) and offer programmes for senior citizens, non-formal education classes, women's development training, medical camps, doctor's visits, and tuition classes for school children,' she says.

'At the Thane Centre, one of our HIV+ children, in spite of her illness and suffering, actively participated in our programmes until the last phase of her life. Her enthusiasm inspired me keep working with gusto. Seeing the alacrity of HIV+ children heartens me to do more for the community. When I hear the laughter of our orphans I feel a great sense of responsibility towards them.' In 2007, Hasina and her team set up the Thane Shelter to provide a safe house for children of sex-workers.

'We now have 30 children residing here. Looking back, Hasina feels proud that she has stayed true to her identity to the extent that she married late, outside of her religion and to a man she knew for a decade. 'I was able to convince my family. In the end I married the man of my choice and I am happy about my decision. Life is beautiful,' says Hasina.

Lakshmi Gautam

Enterpriser and visionary

Founder, Lakshmi Gyan Samaj Seva Sanstha

Kumhrawan near Kanpur in Uttar Pradesh is named after *kumhars* or clay potters who once inhabited the village. The art and process of pottery making involves stretching a ball of clay to create a form which the potter then centers with the wheel. Lakshmi Gautam was possibly wired with this collective unconscious within her to create a legacy of her own, finding her center at the tender age of fourteen.

Raised in a family of seven sisters and a brother, Lakshmi realized early that her parents were not wealthy. She longed to earn money to ease their burden. So while still in school, Lakshmi took her hobby and passion: sewing to new heights. Along with her sister, Lakshmi stitched school uniforms to sell. Her first enterprise proved successful and Lakshmi contributed to the household expenses. Two years later, Lakshmi sought to learn a new skill set. She signed up for a three-month beautician's course at the Gyan Samaj Seva Sanstha in the neighbouring district some 15 kms away. Over the months she was inspired by the director of the institute, Seema Dubey. At her convocation, Lakshmi mustered her courage to talk to Seema. 'I told her, "I want to be like you," and those words simply fell out my mouth,' recalls Lakshmi. Impressed by her chutzpah, Seema asked Lakshmi to gather twenty-five children to teach the skills she had learned in her course. 'But only a few kids could afford the fee of 370 rupees. Most of them could not afford the amount. My mother sold her jewellery to raise 3,400 rupees so I could subsidize the fee for the poorer children. I taught my first group of students and at their convocation when I handed out their certificates, I saw that they were signed by Seema Dubey on behalf of her institute. I asked her what I needed to do to print my name on future certificates.'

Seema advised Lakshmi to register an NGO. Lakshmi says, 'To raise money for the lawyer's fee of 4,000 rupees, my sister and I pooled our scholarship money of 2,500 rupees and my father sold his bicycle for 1,500 rupees. We found out five months later that the lawyer had swindled us.' Determined to set up her NGO, Lakshmi reached the Registrar's office 50 kms away. 'The registrar heard me out and offered to help us at no extra cost and even offered to pay my bus fare on the condition that I would learn everything there was to know about setting up and running an NGO. I complied and attended his training for three months and learned a great deal,' she says.

In 2007, Lakshmi Gyan Samaj Seva Sanstha became operational with an aim to offer women-centred courses. 'For the students to value our services, we had to charge a fee. We first offered a beautician's training course and then added fashion designing, tie-and-dye techniques, embroidery, jewellery making and more. 'Between 2008 and 2009, Lakshmi updated her skill set and while she conducted courses at her institute, she finished her schooling and completed a one year course in computers.

Lakshmi's NGO now has eight branches in neighbouring districts and employs twelve women. So far she has trained 10,000 people through her programmes. Concurrently she has enrolled for a master's in Business Administration Programme through distance education. 'My earnings are paltry. I have a standing in society and the unending support of my parents and sisters, but little in my pocket.' She hopes to raise funds to establish ten such institutes where her students can become teachers too.

लक्ष्मी ज्ञान समाज सेवा संस्थान

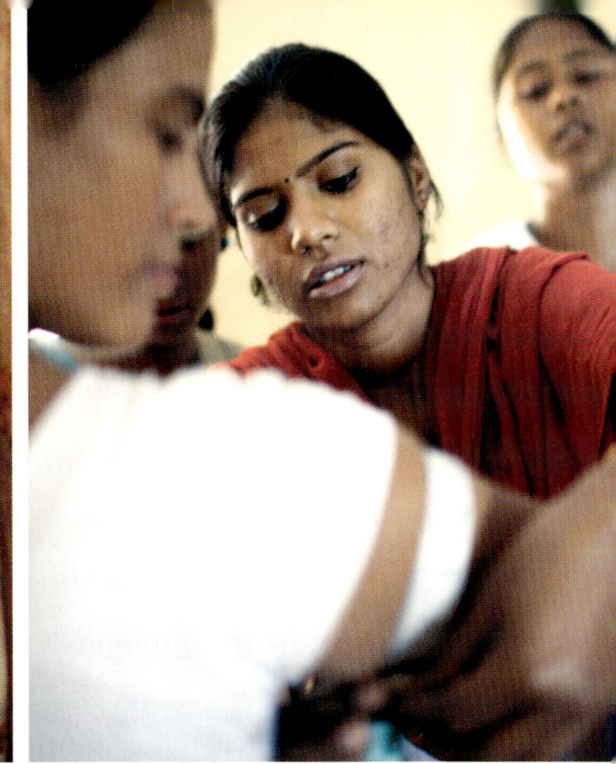

Seat No : 000XXXX
Semester : 5

Indu Shahani

Teacher and liberator

Dean, HR College of Commerce and Economics, Former Sheriff of Mumbai

The turning point in my life came after I appeared for my final year master's in commerce examination and was offered a teaching job at a leading college in Mumbai. At that point of time, I was inclined to accept a lucrative corporate job in one of the foremost FMCG companies in the country. I worked very hard at applying and undergoing a series of gruelling interviews and was all set to join the corporate world. It was something my mother said to me at that time that changed the course of my life. My mother's wise counsel reiterated my faith in the power of education. She said: 'The returns you will get from the smiles of the students will go beyond selling soap, shampoo, and detergent.' Her words touched my heart and at that moment I knew I was destined to be in the field of education.

Since then, there has been no looking back. It has been over three decades since I have been a teacher and an active administrator of higher education. Being in a class, surrounded by young, enthusiastic students gives the teacher a high that no other profession can. Their enthusiasm and energy is infectious and has kept me involved in student activities. With changing technology, the dynamics of academics have changed, but a teacher continues to play an important role in guiding students towards achieving their dreams. While teaching has been extremely rewarding, administering education has always been a challenge. One has to battle against all odds like regulations, faculty mindsets, parent expectations, and bench-marking quality levels and raising them to meet global standards.

As a Dean, I have received a lot of support from the community, corporates, faculty, parents, and students themselves. During my first year as Principal of the H.R. College of Commerce and Economics, we faced problems with admissions, which led me to seek help from the students to improve the admission process. The student think-tank came up with innovative models and the experiment was very successful. For over a decade now, college admissions and a lot of other administrative functions in my college are performed independently by students, with great results. Student empowerment and faculty development have been the key contributors of enhancing quality education besides fostering academia-industry partnerships.

The teaching profession has been very complimentary to my marriage and family life. The support of my husband and in-laws has been instrumental to the success of my career. With my husband being from the corporate world, it has helped me to effectively combine theory with practice, leading me to do my research and Ph.D in academia-industry linkages to enhance higher education. My family has taught me to determine priorities. As a young boy, my son would accompany me very often to college and would sit up nights with me while I evaluated my exam papers. Little did I realize, that one day he would set-up a prominent design school and carry on the family tradition of increasing access to education.

Over the years, experience has taught me that one's own empowerment really does come from empowering others, and in my case empowering my students and their teachers. This has brought about amazing results and a stage has been reached where a process of reverse mentoring has set in, and I am consistently motivated and inspired by my students.

Pooja Bansal

Breaking the barriers of tradition

Owner and Designer, Denotation Design

'In my family, nobody invested in girls. After all, they said, girls have to go to another house; and all they need to know is how to keep it well.' Pooja Bansal, 35, says this with a laugh. Not because she thinks it is funny, but because in her case, it is completely untrue. She grew up needing to know more, to be someone. She comes from a well-to-do and educated background. However, her strict, Marwari upbringing in an Ahmedabad-based business family meant staying within the confines of societal norms. Her future was mapped out for her. A little education, an early marriage, and a life spent taking care of her husband and children's needs. Through sheer persistence, Pooja followed her dream of studying further. She secretly applied to colleges, one of which was the School of Planning and Architecture – one of the best professional colleges of its kind in India. When she got in, her parents were reluctant, but when told by others that it was too good an opportunity to pass up, they relented. 'Things somehow always fell into place,' says Pooja. 'My college was just down the road from our house. And Ahmedabad is a relatively safe city for women. So my parents were less worried.'

She got support from an unexpected quarter. Her mother, who had only studied till grade twelve, smoothed the way with Pooja's father and brother, who were more susceptible to society's demands. 'When I had to go to Goa for my training, my mother convinced my father that I should go. She said to me, "just live your life". 'Following her graduation, the next hurdle was her decision to have a career. She was expected to get married at 23, but she managed to keep going till she was the grand 'old' age of 32. 'I never realized how tough it was for my parents. They faced the social pressure much more than I did. Having an unmarried, working daughter was virtually unheard of in our circles.' Pooja was the first girl in her family to have a job outside the home. Now her sister and a few cousins have followed in her footsteps, but there is a long way to go, yet. 'It's very deep-rooted in my family for the women to stay within the four walls,' she says sadly. In the meantime, she started her own firm. 'I got into business because of a government project that was offered to me in 2000, just after I had graduated as an interior design consultant. The project never took off, but my company, Denotation, did. There was no Godfather, no family contacts, it was just my 'to do' attitude and confidence which kept getting me the initial work,' says a proud Pooja. Now, 13 years later, her company does work across Delhi and Ahmedabad. Their core area is residential design. She explains, 'Designing homes for people has become a passion. My designs incorporate the values I grew up with, that a house needs to be a home. And my strength is the personal touch I add to the homes I make.' Now the company has also ventured into commercial design and hotel interiors. Pooja elaborates on her work philosophy: 'I spend a lot of time with clients, observing them, understanding their lifestyles and unique requirements. And then I reflect these observations in my design, which is the part I absolutely love.'

She now lives in Delhi, married to someone her parents found for her, but who understands and appreciates who she is. Her future plans include starting an online business based on her love of handicrafts and local arts. She teaches value education to children, does art appreciation courses, and is working on evolving her spirituality. And are her parents proud of her? She laughs. 'My family never took what I do seriously. It was only very recently that they even saw one of my houses for the first time. It is only when people called them and told them they love my work, that they realized this was not a hobby for me! 'In 2005, Pooja was shortlisted as one of the fifty top women entrepreneurs of her state.

Nirmala Misra

A magnanimous journey

Teacher and Principal

Imagine a city girl, brought up in a propertied family, exposed to culture and highly-educated, working as the principal of Jauhari Inter College in Lucknow. Now imagine her transported, just months after getting married, to a remote village where her home is a mud hut with a *charpoy* (cot), infested with mosquitoes, with no running water or electricity? Imagine that the first time she wants to use the toilet, she is handed a *lota* (mug), and led off with the rest of the women to an orchard?

Most women would have crumbled, run away, or simply refused to put up with the situation. But Nirmala Misra was different. Without protest, she followed her idealistic husband, Dr. S.B. Misra, who in turn was following his dream of setting up a village school in the most backward area of Uttar Pradesh he could find, leaving behind his handsomely paid career as a geologist in Canada. This was in 1972. 'The area was so primitive. The women would not even come to the door to talk!'

'There was no school for miles around when we came, no means of education,' says Nirmala. Now, more than 40 years later, the village school has grown from the little brick hut measuring 40 feet by 10 feet it started off as.

It has finally received recognition till grade twelve, and has 800 students. Thousands of children, both girls and boys, mostly from scheduled castes, have studied here. This achievement is credited, in large part, to Nirmala Misra. As principal of the school, she taught people from neighbouring villages about the importance of education for their children. Nirmala modestly says, 'We gave just a little encouragement to the women and the scheduled caste families to send their children to school, and were able to make a difference in their thinking.'

Her gentle demeanour and wise counsel changed people's minds forever. She put forward a willing ear and a strong shoulder for their problems and issues. Suddenly, people who initially thought the idea of educating girls was laughable, were sending their daughters to her school. Other people from higher castes, saw the integrity with which the school was run, and soon, children of various social hierarchies were studying side by side. The school started with a total of 100 students, which was no small achievement. 'Since then, so many children have graduated from our school, and gone on to make something of their lives,' she says with pride. 'The girls who have studied with us since kindergarten even convinced their families to let them work further.'

She still remembers the first year when the area got flooded during the monsoon. Nirmala, her husband and another teacher had to wade through knee-deep water to get to school. Her husband wondered whether this would be the last straw for her. However, Nirmala rose to the occasion and began to carry a spare set of clothes to change into at school. Soon, from the epithet initially given to her, 'Canada-*wali-bhabhi*' (sister-in-law from Canada), she began to be seen as a person in her own right, rare for a woman in rural India at the time. She began to be called Principal Sahiba.

Besides running the school, Nirmala started several community activities – singing, theatre, skits, building a bond with the villagers. 'In the beginning, I was accused of being a family planning agent, and had to withstand insults in many ways. Now, when I stand on the village street, a hundred women come out just to talk to me. It is my inner happiness that brings me here everyday ...a happiness I would never have experienced if I had been teaching in the city.'

√324965 = 570.05701
√768945 = 876.89509
11-05-1862 => Sunday
18-04-1919 => Friday
√253968 = 503.952379

Priyanshi Somani

The mental calculator

Student

At an age where most children are playing with dolls, Priyanshi Somani was making friends with numbers. At age six, her mother noticed her prowess in maths, and began to encourage it. 'Once, when I was eight, there was a flood in our area. There was water upto the second floor. I had nothing to do, no school, no TV. So I just did maths, for 10-12 hours. That's the hardest I ever worked.'

By age 10, Priyanshi had won the International Olympiad of Mathematics. In 2010, she had conquered the pinnacle of global mathematical success: winning the Mental Calculation World Cup in Germany. Imagine, 37 geniuses from 16 different countries, some as old as 60, brought to their knees by a 12-year-old Gujarati girl in 6.28 minutes. That is faster than most of us would take to enter the digits in a calculator. Priyanshi solved 10 assigned tasks of finding square roots in the above time. She was the only participant with a 100 per cent accurate answer record for addition, multiplication, and square root in all four of these world cups. She was also the first Indian to win the cup.

What defines genius? Is it merely an in-born talent, or is it brought to the fore by stoking it, nurturing it? Priyanshi says, 'Backed by my parents' support and convictions, I have attained a lot in life. I have had good people supporting me like my teachers. But I know this is only the beginning – I have far to go yet.' Like every other little girl, Priyanshi loves to play games. She loves chess and table tennis, literature, and computers. But she also loves making up maths puzzles that confound most people. 'I create competitive games to sharpen my skills and make it fun. Sometimes, I used to look at my friends playing and feel like I wanted to play too – then I realized I enjoyed maths so much, it was like playing to me!' Making maths fun is something Priyanshi believes passionately. '"Try it" I say to each and every child,' she smiles. She actively promotes the World Maths Day, which she became the Indian ambassador for in 2011.

Affectionately called 'the mental calculator', this 15-year-old shows no boastful immodesty. Instead she is pleasant and confident, ready to face her next challenge. ('It's the regional Maths Olympiad. It's open for kids upto grade twelve, so I will have to work hard.') She is unfazed by the huge media attention she receives in print and on television, locally as well as nationally. Even when her world record in the Mental Calculation cup was broken, she was not deterred. Instead, she set a new world record for the fastest calculation of square roots. Interestingly, she has obviously used her considerable brainpower into investigating her own abilities. She says, 'When a maths problem is in front of you, many processes go on in your mind. From the eye seeing the problem, the brain analyzing it and trying to solve it in the least possible time, and finally putting it on the paper or screen. Challenging the speed of this cycle is what fascinates me. Making a new record is the target, every time.'

It is not clear where Priyanshi's brilliance comes from, her memory, sheer speed of thought, or a genetic advantage. But what is obvious is that she is far from a nerdy, introverted child who will keep her genius to herself. Instead, one senses a well-adjusted teenager, interested in life beyond her own milieu, raring to go ahead and push her limits to make the world a better place. Surprisingly grown up, she says, 'To me this is not "it". It's just a ladder. Right now my plan is to get into the Indian Institute of Technology. After that, I don't know. I am not interested in making a lot of money... but I want to do something for India, something new and original.'

Safeena Husain

The gender equalizer

Founder and CEO, Educate Girls

The London School of Economics and Political Science (LSE) is one of the foremost social science universities of the world. It was founded in 1835 for the 'betterment of society'. Safeena Husain, a stellar graduate from LSE, imbibed not just the School's philosophy but has gone on to create a veritably 'better society' in the villages of Thar Desert. That, however, is not where Safeena's story begins. After studying at LSE, she moved to San Francisco to work with an internet start-up. Alongside, she volunteered with a healthcare NGO on weekends. Her full-time employment ended after a short stint and Safeena bookmarked another path for herself, one that drew her closer to final goal. She chose to travel to Latin America, Africa, and Asia to work with rural and marginalized communities. Her passion ignited and soon enough she felt the need to return to India.

On her return Safeena was deeply impacted by the plague of illiteracy in the country. She says, 'India has the largest illiterate population in the world. Unfortunately, most of the people who lack education are women living in rural areas.' Safeena found her calling and committed herself to empowering her community. Professionally, she shifted gears from health to education.

In 2007, Safeena zeroed in on Rajasthan and in particular the districts of Pali and Jalore to commence her mammoth task of enrolling and retaining girls in schools. The state of Rajasthan earns its disrepute as having 9 out of 26 gender-gap districts in the country, and an alarming figure of 68 per cent of its girls being married as child brides. The causative factors are interlinked: low standard of education, poverty, limiting attitudes towards gender roles, and a lack of support from parents and communities. Safeena says, 'When you educate girls, you can unlock the girl effect dividend, leading to healthier individuals and families, better income and higher returns to society. As a development professional, this is something I feel passionately about.' Safeena's passion, fueled by a deep desire to serve the female population, was enough reason to establish Educate Girls in 2007, an NGO with a vision to 'reform government school education for girls by leveraging existing community and government resources'.

Her business model is both enterprising and reformist. Educate Girls identifies school dropouts to bring them under its ambit, identifies and trains youth volunteers to champion its cause and become 'Team Ballika', and works in consonance with government schools towards a common goal. 'We ensure that the government, teachers, parents, and even girls become active participants in the process and operate independently in school governance even after the withdrawal of Educate Girls,' says a beaming Safeena.

Safeena's Educate Girls has made huge strides in its capacity building efforts in Rajasthan. It covers 495,210 children from 4,500 schools in the Pali and Jalore districts of the state. Over 20,000 girls have been brought back to school while 8,227 girls trained as leaders. In Pali, 88 per cent of the out-of-school girls in this district are now back in school and learning through engaging techniques. Mind-boggling numbers were achieved in five years at just 100 rupees per girl per year! Safeena's 20-year vision is to empower 100 districts in Asia with the highest gender disparity. Her immediate task is to replicate her programme in the Sirohi district. As Asia's 21 Young Leader in 2011, with recognition from Edel Give Social Innovator Honors, and the Village Capital Award, she remains a humanitarian at heart. Safeena Husain continues to create a 'better society'.

B for BRIDE
Saffron
MAARUTI

M for
MARRIAGE
educate girls
टीम बालिका

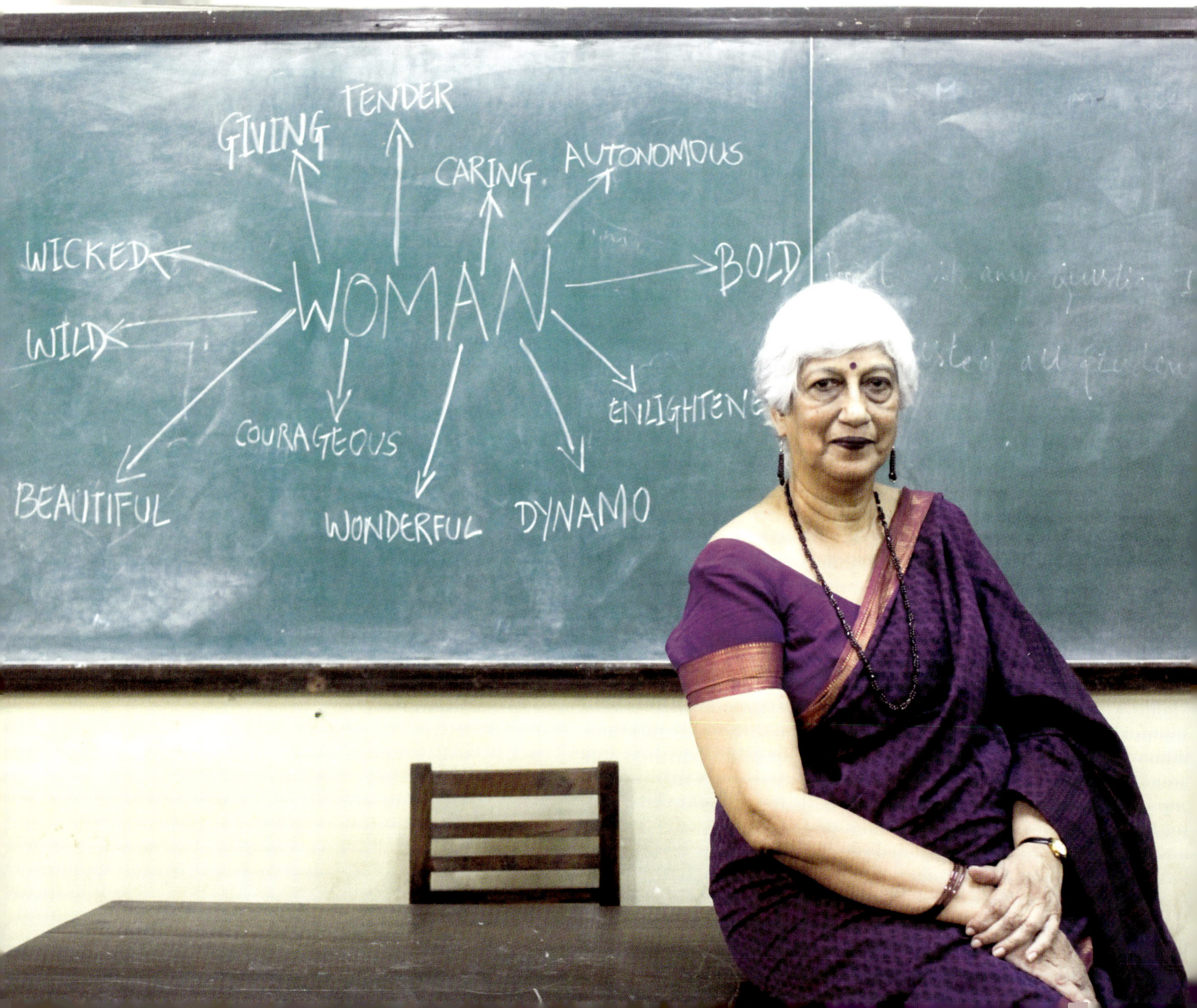

GIVING
TENDER
CARING
AUTONOMOUS
WICKED
WOMAN
BOLD
WILD
COURAGEOUS
BEAUTIFUL
WONDERFUL
DYNAMO

Nandini Sardesai

Thriving on the intangibles

Educator and Activist

Where do I begin and what does one say about oneself? I feel a little diffident and humbled on being asked to write a semi-autobiographical essay. It has been a rather long journey and is a vicarious experience recalling memories, bitter and sweet.

My father was a police officer, so I was brought up with discipline and a strong sense of moral values. We were two sisters, and sometimes, I would overhear chuckles of sympathy for my parents for not having a son. I was hardworking and determined to excel in academics. I would cry if I lost my first place in class. As I had an impressive track record, all my relatives thought I should become a doctor since this was the stereotyped role for a clever (sic) female. But I fell in love with a dashing cricketer and got married at 18. My teachers thought I would give up and I received little encouragement to pursue higher studies except from my darling husband. I did not hesitate to take up the challenge. It was not easy juggling the responsibilities of married life and being a student. Cricketers in the 1960s were paid a meagre 500 rupees for a Test Match. Both my husband and I used the bus to go to our workplaces. We lived in a small, three-room flat. Life was not easy but wedded bliss spurred me on. In my final year, I got pregnant and had my son, Rajdeep and graduated that same year!

I eventually became a fulltime mother, and by the age of 25, had a daughter to take care of. It was at that stage when a chance meeting with Sister Colombier made me rethink my future and I decided to do my B.Ed. I was fortunate to have a mother-in-law who stayed with me for that year since the children were very young. Meanwhile my husband, Dilip had taken up a job in a private business firm since cricket still did not offer adequate remuneration. Our lifestyle improved and our children were given an excellent, all-round education. Meanwhile, I did my master's and started teaching at my Alma Mater, St Xavier's. There were ups and downs, highs and lows along life's pathway with the vicissitudes of fortune but we as a family were there for each other. That is what I think matters in life's journey.

Soon the nest was empty and I wanted to make every moment count as I self-actualized my potential. The opportunity came when I took up cudgels to fight for gender parity at the Bombay Gymkhana which was the bastion of colonial patriarchy. I had to endure many a bitter chauvinistic barb and this battle went on for two years. The war was won with unexpected help from enlightened males. Yes, women all over the world and especially in India, suffer from a plethora of indignities and abuse. Not only do they need to fight back with grit, they also need to be tough and enlist the support of men. The essence of empowerment is not giving up, reaching out, caring and sharing, understanding, tolerance, having empathy and sensitivity. I underwent the trauma of losing my husband when I was not even 63. Even now as I live alone, I am coming to terms with his loss yet I live life on my own terms.

The material accolades for my teaching are minimal but it is the intangibles that give me a sense of satisfaction. Many of my students have accomplishments to their credit, and some of them have not only been in touch but have become good friends. Indeed my mentees are my lifeline and whenever I encounter them, I feel good. Even after retiring I continue to teach as visiting faculty and keep myself occupied in activities as a feminist and an activist. As I scan what I have written, I see I have glossed over the sad bits and focussed on the positive. That is how it should be. Today I have wonderful grandchildren, my children are beautiful human beings.

Sanjeevani Mali

Hope and community

Self Help Group Interventionist

Sanjeevani Mali was married at the age of 16, and ever since, she managed home and hearth. In 2005, the Self Help Group (SHG) movement came to the Katgaon village of Tuljapur district in Maharashtra. Sanjeevani, along with a group of women, established a SHG and became its president. This was a milestone moment for a grade seven dropout. Sanjeevani was clueless when she was required to open a bank account for the SHG, and she was quite baffled by the process.

'It was the beginning of my entry into the world of financial institutions and their complicated procedures,' recalls Sanjeevani. Even though the initial learning challenged Sanjeevani, she persevered and stepped out into the world. 'I acquired a great deal of guidance and education about the operations of the mahila gram panchayats, government schools and hospitals of Swayam Shikshan Prayog (SSP). I was then able to transfer my learning to the management of our SHG, and soon thereafter picked up the confidence to set up a grocery retail shop.'

Running her own venture required Sanjeevani to interact with and seek support from district officials and this helped her to network and imbibe critical life-skills. 'I became a popular entrepreneur in my village and thereby earned a great deal of goodwill. This recognition further boosted my confidence and I registered for the Zila Parishad (district level body) election,' she says. 'The member of the Legislative Assembly who interviewed me was greatly impressed by my work and promptly offered me a nomination ticket to contest the elections. Sanjeevani credits Godavari, Naseem, and Prema among other members of the SSP for honing her skills. 'Their support enabled me to travel extensively within Maharashtra, and also to Delhi to train aspiring entrepreneurs and share our vision with others. All the training programmes have been rewarding and I always returned to my SHG with invaluable insights. Our group has galvanized the formation of 40 SHGs in our village.'

Sanjeevani and her SHG's interventions have served the needs of the villagers of Katgaon in several spheres. She has implemented programmes on organic composting methods for farmers who largely cultivate sugarcane and grapes as cash crops. 'Our SHGs trained in Nanded, Satara, and Boramani to specifically cater to these farmers as both the crops are water-intensive and demand large quantities of fertilizer. We inducted 100 farmers and educated them in organic composting techniques. They benefitted greatly and went on to constitute a group of their own called Swayam Nirman Community, and half its members now practice horticulture.' Sanjeevani's SHGs implement government schemes in inclusive and comprehensive ways. 'Eighty per cent of our girls go to school and get married at the age of 18 or after. We offer medical check-ups, and nearly all children are vaccinated for polio. We are proud to say that six kindergarten schools, one senior school, two English-medium schools, and a government hospital are some of the facilities we have.'

Perhaps the most innovative and prudent alternative to unaffordable lavish weddings for the village folk is the organization of mass marriages in the Taluka headquarters on specific dates. 'We organized the first such event in 2005, and several couples have opted to wed this way to avoid extravagant expenses. Furthermore, couples receive a token gift of 1,000 rupees from the community. We hope our village elders lead the way with this campaign so we may eradicate the social evil of dowry.' Sanjeevani Mali marches on with determination, ameliorating lives and being the change.

Usha Prajapati

Daring to dream

Crafts Entrepreneur

'I found India's best design institute to be hell.' Usha Prajapati went to the National Institute of Design (NID), Ahmedabad, without knowing a word of English. How she overcame that obstacle is a true story of heroism and will power. The daughter of a car mechanic from Bihar, the youngest of seven children, she grew up with few benefits other than a father who worked hard to give her an education, and of course, he had firm faith in her talent and potential.

Getting into NID was a dream come true. But for a girl from a Hindi-medium school, it was hard to fit in. Depressed and disheartened, Usha had nearly given up, when something within her awoke. 'I am a dreamer – a believer of "doing good and doing well". Slowly I gathered the courage and realized that the only mantra in life was to work hard and be honest.' This change in attitude propelled Usha into finishing her course, and graduating from NID with a diploma in textile design in 2003.

But Usha was not satisfied. 'This was just the beginning; I wanted to explore my full potential and touch the sky.' In 2006, she was awarded the Ford Foundation's International Fellowship, and went on to get a master's degree in International Development and Social Change from Clark University, USA in 2008.

Usha's chosen field was the creation of livelihood-generating opportunities for local communities, or 'livelihood project design & implementation'. 'I wanted to help young girls who dared to come out of their cocoon and the closed mindsets around them to learn something in life.'

It was on a trip to visit her parents in Gaya, Bihar, that she began to realize that it was important not to forget where one came from, and to give back to that place. 'I strongly believe that each of us who are educated and privileged have certain responsibilities towards our roots, the place where we are born,' she explains. This was the origin of her organization Samoolan, which means 'giving back to your roots'.

A grassroots NGO, Samoolan works with women in the local area and helps them with social entrepreneurship and income generation activities. The idea is to make the women financially independent, and thus, empowered. Usha says proudly, 'Samoolam is a self-sustaining organization without any external funding or support.' The initiative simultaneously provides employment for women as well as promoting the crochet craft of the area, which was dying out. The products are marketed all over the country. Like many projects of its kind, it was difficult to begin with – most of the women faced objections from their families or spouses; some even left the training halfway. But soon, as the women who remained in the group started making money, several of the original members returned to the fold. 'At present, Samoolan engages more than 70 women from Gaya who are earning their own living. And not to forget, they are building the crafts identity for this region,' says Usha.

And as for Usha, she has a clear vision and she is working hard to get to it. As she looks back, she feels she has been very lucky. 'I was following my dreams and new paths and directions were getting paved slowly with time. I feel privileged to have family and well-wishers supporting me.'

Vidya Joshi

Philanthropic perseverances

Self Help Group Initiator and Social Entrepreneur

Vidyatai, as she is affectionately known, chose to work for her community out of a burning desire to make a difference in the lives of people. For over 15 years now, Vidya has been serving women in the villages of the Nanded district in Maharashtra, selflessly and with benevolence. Born to a well-to-do Brahmin family, Vidya was nurtured and loved through her years and was encouraged to complete school. She was keen to study further but could not because of the lack of facilities for graduate studies. When she was 20, her parents married her off to a man called Gopalrao in Sonkhed and she began to lead the life of a householder. All the while, Vidya had persistent thoughts of reaching out to the womenfolk in her neighbourhood and village.

In 1997, Vidya first learned about Self Help Groups (SHGs) from a member of the Maharashtra Rural Credit Project (MRCP) and she instinctively felt drawn towards the initative. With consent and support from her family, Vidya formed the first SHG in Sonkhed. Appreciated by the members of her group and rewarded by the experience she gained, she went ahead and created several more such groups and became accomplished in replicating the self-governance model. 'Serving my community gives me great joy. I like what I do even though it involves commuting across 15 villages by bus, auto or foot,' says Vidya.

In a short span of two years, Vidya has successfully established 25 SHGs, taking under her wing over 200 women and empowering them to execute bank transactions, seek financial assistance and set up small businesses to support their families. Vidya saw potentially talented women in her groups and urged them to make products like handicrafts, food items, and decorative pieces to sell in nearby districts and at exhibitions through stalls. She organized a collection of such products to market at the National Bank for Agricultural and Rural Development's (NABARD) farmer's meet in Pune and the effort was met with great success. NABARD recognized Vidya's efforts and awarded her for her contribution towards the development of women and movement of SHGs. Vidya says, 'It was a great honour to receive this award from Member of Parliament Supriya Sule. I have also received awards from the Tehsil and district administration for excellence in managing SHGs.'

One of Vidya's most outstanding contributions to her village was putting an end to the rampant practice of open defecation. 'I initiated a door-to-door campaign in my village to explain the detrimental effects of open defecation. I was able to solicit support of the Gram Sabha and we built five toilets for 8,000 rupees,' she says. Vidya was acknowledged yet again with a letter of commendation.

In 2012, Vidya moved her attention to women farmers in the Loha tehsil. She has formed 15 SHGs which systematically evaluate, communicate and disseminate the best practices of sustainable agriculture. Her own sustainability comes from a general supplies shop she owns. 'I live a happy life with my husband. I have four daughters who are married and working and I, for one, understand the value of education for the girl child. I would very much like every human being to seriously encourage the inherent will power and strength within a woman. With our capabilities we can change society,' says Vidya. She dreams of enabling all girls with the ability to acquire a higher education. Vidya is a woman and she can make it happen.

The **Leaders**

'Do not wait for leaders,
do it alone, person to person.'

Mother Teresa

Anita Rana

The homemaker activist

Director, Janhit

When Anita Rana's husband died of a sudden heart attack, she knew that she could not let his dreams and his passion go waste. So, this unassuming housewife took over the reins of Janhit, the NGO her husband Anil Rana had founded and run since 1998. 'I did not even know what an NGO did,' she says candidly. 'When I saw my husband at work, changing people's lives, his face would light up. I didn't understand this then – but I do now.'

She understands it – because under her, Janhit has had a far-reaching impact, largely in the area of promoting organic farming through the use of bio-pesticides and organic manures in western Uttar Pradesh, known for its dependence on standard fertilizers. Janhit has started the first ever organic ingredients outlet in Meerut. They also focus on rainwater harvesting programmes, having established them in 10 schools, and in 70 buildings in Meerut. 'We have programmes where we use Corporate Social Responsibility funds to conserve traditional water bodies. We evoke the idea of community ownership, so that people themselves help in sustaining them. We remind people that their ancestors bathed in the very same water bodies, and appoint *jalbhais* and *jalbehens* (male and female custodians) to take the responsibility of their upkeep.'

In the beginning, she was discouraged by people for taking up her husband's work. 'They told me that I was a housewife and could only manage my house, not an NGO. Even my children complained that I wasn't home enough for them. People find it hard to accept that a woman, a single one especially, can achieve something.' But slowly, as her confidence grew, and her leadership of Janhit and its projects produced results, she started being taken seriously. Her education projects for young people on conserving the environment are extremely successful.

However, her work with women and children is what is closest to her heart. 'I have noticed the special connection that women have with water. We get them involved in water conservation efforts because after all, the lack of water affects them the most. And it is the women who think about the grassroots issues, they have a holistic perspective. Their opinion is very important. We have started several programmes where we encourage women farmers, and recognize their contribution to their family's income through domestic chores as well as agricultural labour, which otherwise usually goes unnoticed.'

Besides environmental issues, Janhit has other ongoing programmes, many of which involve advocacy and increasing access to, and awareness about government schemes for the poor and disadvantaged. Janhit runs a children's helpline, and works with children who live in Meerut's vast slums, giving them informal education which leads to admission in government schools. They also engage with mothers to promote health initiatives. Anita reminisces, 'It was difficult, coming out of a 21-year period of doing only household work, having to give up wearing a *pallu*... but the memory of my husband inspired me... and it was all for a good cause. My children are proud of me now and that feels very good.' She has travelled all over the world, and her contributions have been widely applauded. Anita's work with Janhit was recognized and awarded by the United Nations Development Programme as well as the Earth Day network in 2012. She continues her work with children and women. 'There are others like me, but they don't have support. If I had not stepped out of my house on the thirteenth day after my husband's death, I would have not been where I am today. I would have been stuck within the four walls of my house, washing and cooking. I am glad I took that step and came out of my comfort zone.'

NUMERICAL CHART
हिन्दी वर्णमाला चार्ट

उद्देश्य

Sports Car
Diamond
Diamond
बेटी बचाओ

Chhavi Rajawat

The MBA sarpanch

Sarpanch, Soda Village

The pretty young girl in jeans is sitting under the shade of an ancient tree in the middle of a village, surrounded by its inhabitants. She is talking earnestly to them. If you look closer, you will notice, that they, man or woman, young or old, are listening to her with rapt attention.

This is just another day in the life of Chhavi Rajawat, Sarpanch of Soda village, Rajasthan. In 2010, Chhavi was approached by the people of the village (which is her native place), to stand for the Panchayat elections. 'My grandfather was the Sarpanch of Soda many years ago, and that was the only time this place saw any development. The villagers have faith in my family. So 50 people came to my house in Jaipur, asking me to stand, because that year there was a women's reserved seat up for grabs. I couldn't say no – the hope and expectations in their eyes did not allow me to.'

And so, Chhavi, who has an MBA, gave up her corporate job and became Sarpanch. Having spent all her vacations in the village, she was familiar with the people and quickly won their trust. She was different in her approach, though. Not affiliated to any political party, she meant to play by the rules. 'I told them, I'll come in, but you may be sorry, because I will play fair... even with people who have voted for me, even if it is my own family.' Chhavi soon realized that her job was going to be monstrously difficult. The village was severely underdeveloped. People lived in the most basic of mud houses. The school was cramped and the teachers few. Electricity only came for a few hours a day. And most fundamental of all was the problem of the scarcity of potable water. The ground water in the region was contaminated and saline, and the people depended mainly on rainwater, which in this drought-prone area was a rarity. She decided to redevelop the reservoir, the traditional catchment area. She approached the government with an exhaustive project proposal. Impressed, the officials told her they would like to help, but she could not use government machinery to de-silt the lake. 'So I have collected some money from family and friends, but I still have a long way to go,' she says. In the meantime, she started looking at other problems in the village such as encroachment and sanitation. She has managed to extend the number of hours electricity is available, and has brought the internet to her people. Chhavi has presented her case to ministers and bureaucrats. She has been to UNICEF to ask for funding for toilets. She has made development visible. 'When people see development, there is a big change in their attitude. We were talking about encroachment. I told them you have to think about the future. Your children will have two wheelers and then four wheelers... if there a the need for an ambulance, we need the required road width. The next day, people had broken down walls of their homes that encroached on public land.'

On 25 March 2011, Chhavi spoke at the UN's 11th Infopoverty World Conference. In her speech she said, 'If India continues to make progress at the same pace as it has for the past 65 years since independence, it just won't be good enough. We'll be failing people who dream about having water, electricity, toilets, schools and jobs. I am convinced we can do it differently and do it faster.' She wants her native Soda to develop holistically and become a model village that can be emulated all over the country. Working in the corporate sector gave Chhavi a certain discipline and training that she uses to manage her work in the village. But it is being a 'daughter of the village' that gives her the empathy and insight to understand issues and their long-term resolution.

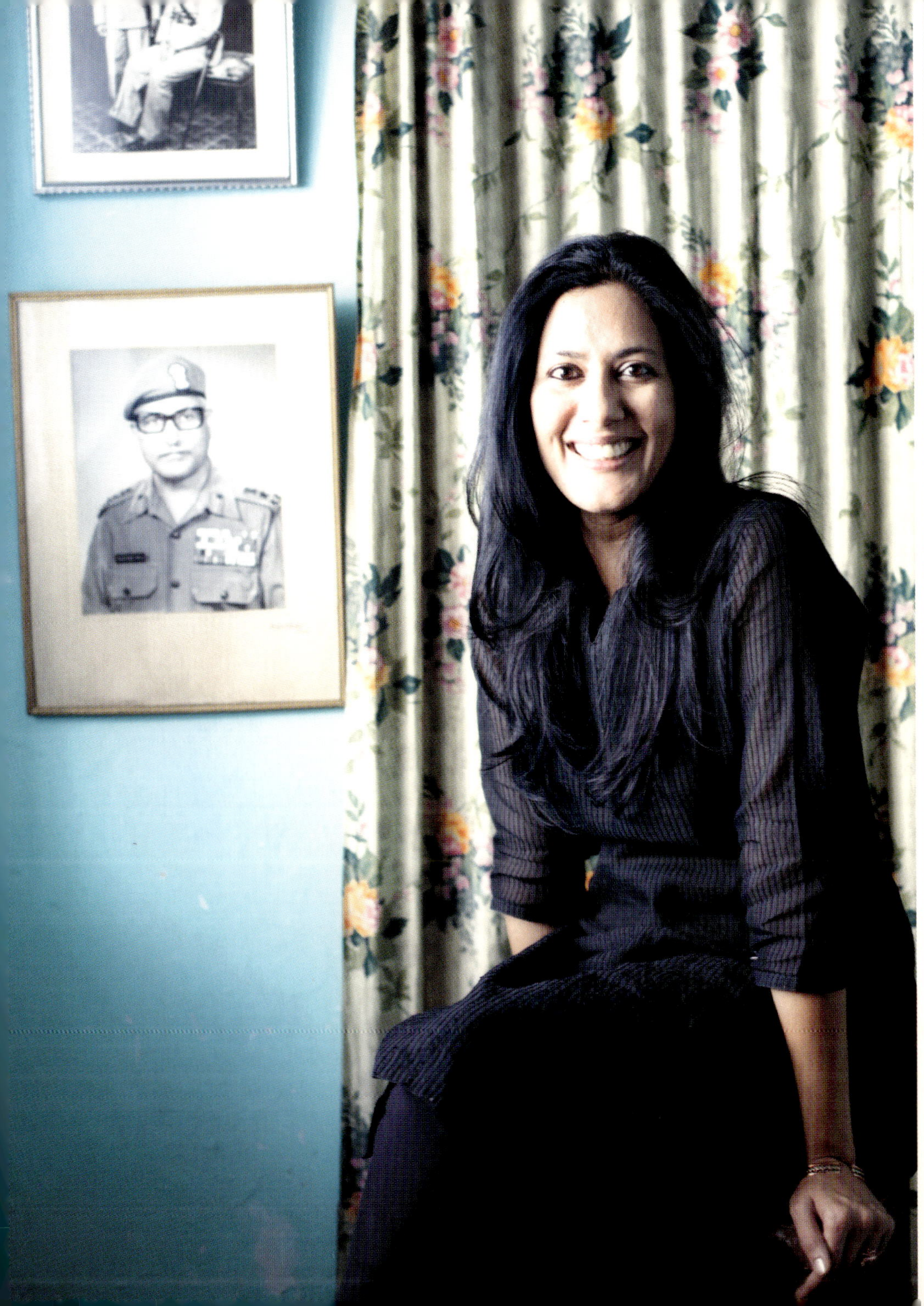

ग्रा.पं. सोडा के जन प्रतिनिधियों की सूची
सरपंच
उप सरपंच
वार्ड पंच

Aruna Roy

Governance begins at the grassroots

Social Activist and Member, MKSS

One cannot normally trace one's life with the history of a country. But as 'midnight's children', born over the cusp of independence, we carry memories of angst. Our political understanding, imbibed through osmosis, underwrites our life. Perhaps mine has been shaped by the senseless killings born out of fear, incited ironically in the name of religion, which should ideally speak of compassion and tolerance. The assassination of Gandhi*ji* horrified India, and stilled the waters for a while.

My childhood was a haven of inclusiveness and equality. My parents brought us up with an understanding of compassion. They taught us the rigour of rationality, transgression of scholastic disciplines, and rejection of social inequality and intolerance. My engagement with social and public action was born out of this understanding of discrimination, whether it was by caste, class, gender, or religion. As a woman, a victim per se, I felt empowered to understand the possibilities of protest and pushing boundaries. The worst of these conditions was poverty and its indignity. The immorality of indifference, disparity, and callousness, made me cringe. My choice of work was rooted in this concern.

My search for meaningful engagement began with a seven-year stint of exposure to governance with the IAS from 1968-75. I began development work in rural India. The nine years I spent with the Social Work Research Centre in Tilonia, Rajasthan, grounded my understanding of discriminatory politics on the cutting edge of our society. I was tutored by great unsung heroes; men and women, who unlettered as they were, understood the politics of their struggle and its limitations. We grew together and my most important gurus in public action came from the villages. Norti, a dalit woman and the recipient of many awards is a symbol for me. Fearless of both caste and class hierarchies, she faced modern challenges, and has now mastered working on a computer. Continuing to live as she did – frugally, working on the National Rural Employment Guarantee Act work sites, she monitors everything on the computer! People like her tether me to a reality, which shakes my cynicism and gives me hope.

It is from this understanding of politics and development that the Mazdoor Kisan Shakti Sangathan (MKSS) was born in 1990, with a collective of a hundred people discussing the nature of public protest to reclaim democracy. This made me shift once again from Tilonia to Devdungri to work amidst people who were poor but willing to struggle. It marked the beginning of a dialectic conversation between struggle and engagement. A leader of the workers provided us with an understanding of democracy and governance from where people actually are, and led us to the definition of the Right to Information Act. As Sushila, from the MKSS, put it succinctly at a press conference in Delhi in 1996, 'If I send my son to the market with ten rupees, when he comes back, I ask for accounts. The Government spends crores of rupees in my name, should I not ask for accounts? *Hamara paisa, hamara hisab* (our money our accounts).'

The demand for the National Rural Employment Guarantee Act is vilified by affluent pundits who grudge the hundred days of work at minimum wages. The promise in 1947 of freedom was not only from the British colonizers. It was also a promise of freedom from hunger and want. The rhetoric of promises made by democracy is being challenged by the poor. If there is hope for this country, it is from the hard work and optimism of these people – Chunni Singh battling want and migration, Meera burdened by debts, Bhils who fought daily hunger and received grain for 6 months, the Saharia who fought bondage and accessed land. They have been effective in making collective change possible and have gone from feudal unquestioning to questioning the state. This promise of democracy is being realized through struggle and facing daily threats of violence.

This transition from acceptance of inequality to questioning it, and legitimizing demand through democratic legislation was shaped by the poor. The RTI Act makes democracy tangible and allows the voter to speak. It exemplifies that small acts of bravery are possible, and these will make the larger wheels turn; it is India's hope for better governance. The journey continues. Amendments to the RTI, fighting discriminatory and communal politics – the horizon will keep shifting.

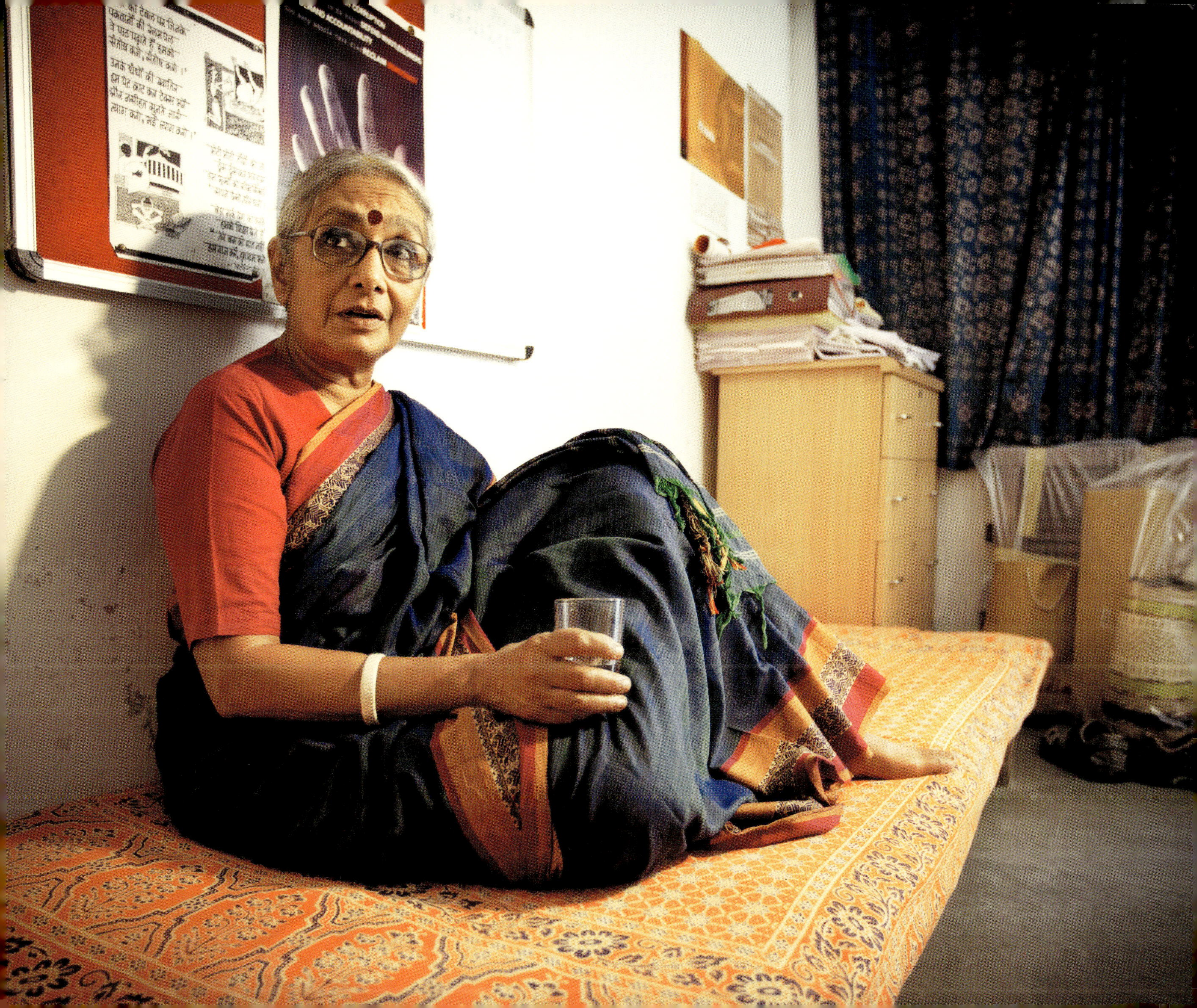

संतोष करो, संतोष करो।
उनके धंधों की खातिर
AND ACCOUNTABILITY

ZP

Godavari Dange

From strength to strength

Social Activist and Self Help Group Establisher

The Godavari basin in Maharashtra is the second largest mangrove forest in the country and it stands firmly at the intersection of land and sea. Nearby lives Godavari Dange in Gandhora village of Osmanabad district, Maharashtra. Not long ago, though, Godavari was an emotionally brittle woman, barely able to sustain herself.

In 1999, Godavari sank into depression following the death of her husband. He left behind two toddler sons and a barely educated, young, fragile widow in a 'dark place'. She wallowed in sadness for a whole year until her mother, a member of a Bachat Gat (savings Self Help Group) prodded at her to attend the group's meetings. At one such meeting, Godavari met an encouraging man, Balasaheb Kaldali of Shikshan Prayog (SSP). He urged her to seek training from SSP to constitute and manage Self Help Groups in and around her village. She took the advice seriously, and in 2000, Godavari established, with the help of SSP, three Self Help Groups in Gandhora.

The groups enabled women to stockpile savings, seek loans, and acquire training to start small businesses. From a despondent homebody, Godavari began to evolve into a self-reliant woman. Godavari soon grasped the dilemmas and obstacles faced by families in neighbouring villages. The scope of her service expanded to encompass women's health, education, gram panchayat, water projects, employment, and surveying business possibilities for women. As secretary of the Tuljapur Taluka Foundation, Godavari launched a drive to recover loan monies from other Self Help Groups. This enabled her to seek a loan of 5 lakh rupees from the bank. 'We bought noodle-making machines and chili powder grinders as business propositions for our women members,' she says.

Godavari shares, 'Big businesses do not thrive in nearby villages. Population numbers are small and people are poor. So women prefer to set up corner stores to sell daily-need items. Over the years, the womenfolk have learnt to save money and are now financially stable, but are strapped for time to consider start-up ventures as they work the fields. Some years ago women could only save 25 rupees per month, but now they can put aside up to 500 rupees per month.' As a powerful representative and voice of rural women, Godavari was selected to speak at the AIDS Conference in Kenya in 2007. 'I liked that the participants talked openly about the epidemic, unlike in our villages,' she says. 'I am now committed to educating women about HIV/AIDS.'

Over the years, Godavari has represented India at the Huairou Commission in Philippines on emergency measures, the Conference on Food Security in Rome, the South Asian Conference in Emergency Facilities in Nepal, and the Women's Conference in the United States of America. 'I thought I was going to Amravati,' she laughs. Godavari has made lasting connections with fellow farmers and grassroots workers across nations. 'I have been able to educate my sons with my earnings. My younger son is in grade ten and my older one is in college studying agricultural engineering.'

This young, sprightly social activist does not make much of her hectic daily schedule that involves travelling 30 to 50 kms each day to meet women in far-flung villages. 'Tomorrow's planning has to be done today,' she says. Godavari epitomizes the force of the river that flows near her village: forceful, strong and evolving.

Mittal Patel

Humanity personified

Social Worker

Mittal Patel, armed with a gold medal in journalism, was on her way to becoming a mainstream scribe, when her middle-class sensibilities were shaken up, her conscience wrung out and a call to action begun. She had stumbled upon a story that would change the course of her entire life. And in turn, her work would alter the lives of thousands of people belonging to the lost tribes of her native Gujarat. 'I came into contact with these nomadic and de-notified tribes during an assignment, and I started looking at their life and condition very closely. I realized, to my horror, that 40 lakh people in Gujarat were living without an identity.'

'When I was a child, people like this used to come to my village to entertain us... some were fire eaters, or acrobats, folk theatre performers, others were knife sharpeners or snake catchers. They fulfilled a role in our society.' But many of these traditional professions soon fell into jeopardy. Snake catchers were reduced to begging after the Wildlife Act banned the snake trade. The entertainers were replaced by electronic media in the public's imagination. Worst of all, they were not even counted in the Census until recently. 'They are perceived as criminals – the only government record they are on is the police station's,' says Mittal. 'They are given no place in society, no official identity of their own.' Mittal realized that the lack of any formal government recognition meant that these people were unable to access basic rights like education and ownership of land, and had no way to benefit from government schemes for the poor.

In 2006, she quit her job and began working full time to ameliorate the lives of such nameless people through Vicharta Samuday Samarthan Manch, or VSSM, her NGO. It was difficult, as the community was understandably mistrustful and shy. But she persevered. She started tent schools that could travel with the nomads. There are now 31 such schools in operation. She began to actively lobby the government to look on them as citizens of India.

'You must be thinking, what's in an ID proof? You just apply and get it after a few months – your ration card, or driver's license, or voter card. But for those people who don't have an address, an ID proof can be your only hope of avoiding jail for a crime you did not commit, because you could not prove your identity.' In 2008, VSSM, along with Gujarat's chief electoral officer gave more than 20,000 people their first address, and their first stamp of being citizens... voter cards. Around 5,000 of them are also gainfully employed.

This young, determined woman, who is universally called Mittalben, or sister Mittal, has formed a network of 22,000 families in 9 districts that she helps. Not surprisingly, at a recent TEDx talk, she said, 'We have gained a lot of friends and well wishers along the way.' Their success is astounding. 'We run 26 alternate schools, where thousands of children are enrolled. We have managed to get 30,000 people an address.' VSSM has organized mass marriages in Vadia village in order to stop the pimping off of young girls who are literally born into the flesh trade as a customary practice. Mittal has helped these marginalized communities procure houses, ration cards, bank accounts, and more. Most impressively, she has managed to get land allotted to these communities so that finally, they have a place of their own to call home.

'We have been in the debt of these communities for generations – they have been a crucial part of society, contributing to it through their professions. It is time to repay that debt to them.'

Canon

Priya Dutt

Not in it for the power

Politician, Member of Parliament

My journey has been a very interesting and an unpredictable one. According to Indian standards, I got married at a late age. But I wanted to wait till I found a partner that I could see myself wanting to grow old with. I married Owen Roncon when I was 36, and everyone around me heaved a sigh of relief, happy to see me finally settling down. Life was bliss, and soon I found out I was pregnant. However, one day I woke up to a life that had changed forever. My father had passed away in his sleep leaving our family directionless. He filled in as a father, a mother, a mentor, a role model, and my hero.

I had worked with him and accompanied him on many of his adventures. But a career in politics was not something I had been groomed for or aspired towards. I had found my own calling which was working for the people, making a difference where I could – and politics at the time did not fit in. I had seen my father's struggles, his frustration, and pain whilst in politics. After the demise of a sitting elected representative, it is mandatory to conduct elections for that constituency within 6 months. After a lot of hesitation, I agreed to stand for election. I was four-months pregnant. I think it was the love and hope I saw in the eyes of the people in my father's constituency that helped me decide to continue the work he had started. I always remember his words, 'I use politics for the right reasons to change society and lives.'

I started by visiting the area and meeting people, so they would get to know me, and at the same time I was advancing with my pregnancy. On 26 July 2005, Mumbai had one of its worst deluges. My work became a lot more intense, organising relief for the affected people. I worked nearly 10 to 12 hours a day. For a while, I forgot I was pregnant. By the time I went to file my nomination, I was carrying a little suitcase with me wherever I went, in case I went into labour. I filed my nomination and then went straight to the hospital and delivered my first-born. Five days later, my campaign began.

Those fifteen days were very difficult. I would campaign from 8 am to 6 pm. I was coming home to feed my baby every two hours, and it was painful to leave him. There were days I wanted to give up. I just wanted to be with my son and hold him and cry – and I did. For me, he embodied hope and I felt like he understood what I was going through. He was a calm and happy baby. And unlike most newborns, he would sleep through the night, giving me time to rest. I faced a lot of challenges in this new world of politics. Here, I was a complete amateur, about to step into my father's position, and that was not taken too well and rightly so. We had a small but strong team, my husband, some friends, well-wishers of my father who had worked with him, and his dedicated office staff. I was able to create my own style of work. I realized that starting with a clean slate would be the best thing. I was honest in my campaign for the people, and won with a margin of more than 1 lakh votes, but the victory was not mine – it was my father's.

After the elections, another challenge I faced was with people who thought I was just a puppet. But they soon realized I can be quite a headstrong and stubborn person. My greatest strength was my lack of hunger in politics. I was in it not for the power or money, but to make a difference and to be able to do some good.

I have tried my best to make my family my priority. My husband and I never leave the children alone. I try to switch off when I am home but sometimes it is difficult. Owen is a rock who I know will always be there if I falter. He is also my biggest critic. We respect each other's work without interfering in it. We have a very normal family life and do things no differently from any other family.

Most people measure the empowerment of a woman in terms of the success she achieves in her career. I don't quite agree with that as I know that a homemaker can be as empowered as a CEO. You are empowered when you stand up for what is right and for what you believe in. It is when you work towards the good of all in any way you can. I feel a sense of fulfillment everyday at work when I am able to put a smile on someone's face or make a difference in someone's life.

43

Noorjahan Kaladigi

Basti builder

Slum and Infrastructure Rehabilitator

Some of the most remarkable, inspiring and touching human stories are about women who show exemplary optimism in the face of poverty, rejection, widowhood, and illiteracy. Noorjahan Kaladigi is one such woman. Not long ago, she led a sheltered life behind her purdah, oblivious of the world around her. A child bride at 12 and a teen mother, Noorjahan was barely 26 when her husband passed on leaving behind two young children in Miraj, Maharashtra.

'My life was contained in my jhuggi and my *basti* was my world. I seldom stepped out and the times when I ventured to the bazaar, I would ride an auto rickshaw pre-arranged by my husband. I saw little of my surroundings from behind my purdah,' she says. 'After my husband's death, my children and I went hungry for a few days. We were left to fend for ourselves. I knew then that I had to be strong. I defied all norms of my community and took up two part-time jobs as a cook. I still remember my first day at work. My body trembled with fear and my employer, a doctor, reassured me by calling me her sister,' recalls Noorjahan. Her confidence increased even as her parents and community castigated her. In six months, Noorjahan dropped her purdah and embraced the *pallu*. For a whole year she was excommunicated by her neighbours and family for losing her veil and bringing dishonour to the community. In 2001, Shelter Associates initiated a slum rehabilitation project in and around Noorjahan's *basti*. 'At first I was suspicious of their intent as no agency had, until then, addressed the problems we faced,' shares Noorjahan. Her neighbours urged her to stop protesting their presence, and when she did, she kindled her own empowerment process. In six months Shelter Associates built 15 blocks of separate toilets for men, women and children with participation from the locals as Noorjahan spearheaded the campaign. 'My neighbours were thrilled and praised my efforts. The toilets changed our lives. Often I would not eat all day as I could not bear to defecate in the open in the day or with car headlights shining on me at night. It was degrading to live like that. I knew I had to reach out to other *basti* dwellers and help them build toilets,' she says.

Shelter Associates recognized Noorjahan's leadership skills and personal strength and absorbed her as a community worker. *Bhabhi* (sister-in-law), as she respectfully came to be called, marshalled the NGO's slum rehabilitation projects. Then in 2004, Noorjahan lost her 17-year-old daughter. 'I was devastated and held my grief in my heart. My loss was a catalyst in a way. I was more determined than ever to do good for others and Shelter Associates supported me all along,' she says. Noorjahan's most challenging project has been the relocation of the Sanjay Nagar slum to a transit camp. The dwellers will be resettled in the upcoming four-storey social housing complex nearby. 'The slum dwellers pointed out that the toilets were permanent structures while the jhuggis were temporary and asked me to change that for them. This plan demanded a great deal of communication with the dwellers, the NGO, and the government departments to initiate a housing project. During the relocation, Shelter Associates asked me to cook meals for the families for three days as the dwellers transitioned. This was my way to foster relationships and build trust,' says Noorjahan.

In 2011, Noorjahan addressed the Women's United Nations meet on gender issues in Delhi. Noorjahan has a message for women who live in slums and in abject poverty, 'You have immense strength. You will be able to become a force to reckon with. Support your children fully, and serve others with genuine compassion.'

Norti Bai

Changing with the times

Sarpanch, Change-Maker and Computer Whiz

An elderly lady dressed in a traditional Rajasthani sari is bent over a table, focused on her work. As you come closer, you gasp. She is not doing elaborate needlework or kneading dough. She is furiously at work on a computer, tapping at the keyboard and skillfully manipulating a mouse over the complicated diagrams on the monitor of the PC.

This incongruous, though uplifting vision is named Norti Bai, who became computer literate at the grand old age of 60. Now, seven years later, she runs computer classes for young girls in her area, even the ones who have dropped out of school. She represents the enlightened thought that the internet is not just for the urban or the elite – it can be a real tool for empowerment.

No one sees this more clearly than Norti. She was introduced to computers through the Barefoot College, an organization for change through learning at the grassroots level, when she was working as a field agent for the Social Work Research Centre, fighting for equal wages for men and women. She found it difficult at first – the manual dexterity required was new to her, and the English was a challenge. But soon, she started working with Hindi software, and then there was no stopping her! She began to see great potential to help her community through computers and their use.

Her first project was to map the water resources in her village, and the neighbouring ones too, as she grasped clearly how precious water was in her arid Rajasthan. Her attitude proved to be another great example of how women, when given resources, will first look towards basic needs of their community before anything else. She galvanized the village women to help her pinpoint and note the location of ponds, wells, tube wells, and other water sources in the area, which they would map and offer to the government so that policy-makers could have true and immediate information.

The project took off. She now has 3,000 women in 250 villages doing these surveys, which she uses to create and maintain a database of the water sources in the region. For her efforts towards rural development, Norti Bai was awarded the CII-Bharti Woman Exemplar Award in 2007. Where does she surf? 'I look at the different Panchayats that are progressing so that I can learn from them,' she says. No time for Facebook, 'work comes first.'

Beloved of the women of her village, and solely responsible for a large part of the literacy of its population, Norti Bai was elected the first dalit woman sarpanch of Harmara village. She has been a guest speaker at conferences and events, including the Conference on Media, IT and Grassroot Development in Bangalore. 'I too thought computers were of no use to villagers, but it is a wrong impression,' she says. She is driven by this knowledge and her faith in the power of education for the progress of her community. The school dropout is a woman on a mission.

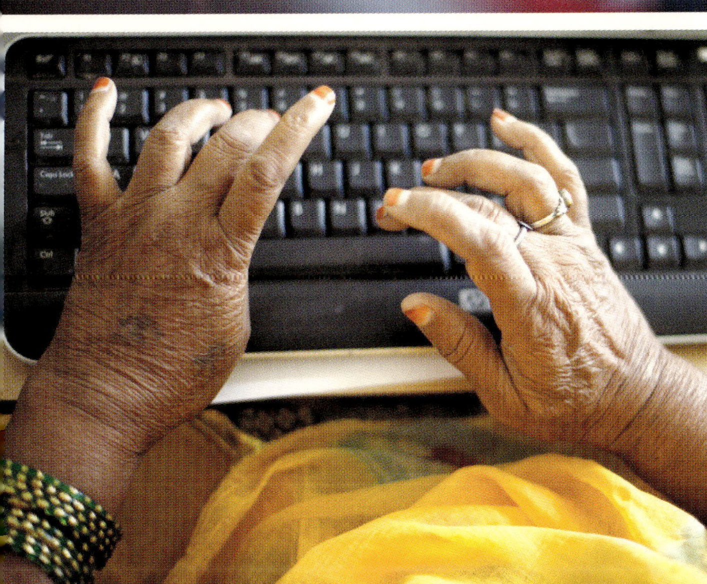

जिला : अजमेर
परिवार राशन कार्ड
जिला : अजमेर
जिला : अजमेर
परिवार राशन कार्ड

Pinky Devi

Rice and shine

Village Resource Person

In 2009, Pinky Devi, a mother of three stepped out from the obscurity of her home and walked into a village Self Help Group (SHG) after coming in contact with Jeevika, an organisation that tackles the roots of poverty and revitalises rural communities.

Pinky joined a Self Help Group (SHG) comprising twelve members, which has over time evolved into a Village Organization (VO) which has ten SHGs. One of its primary objectives was to shut down alcohol retail shops, which it successfully did. A year later, Pinky volunteered to be a Village Resource Person (VRP) and wanted to impact agriculture in her area. She went on to receive training from the Jeevika Trust on the System of Rice Intensification (SRI) and its benefits.

In fact, Pinky and some members of her SHG were a few of the first adopters of SRI in their village Nahub (Bihar). Pinky adopted SRI on her own land, following which she visited every member of the VO to explain how this method would improve yield and reduce costs. As a result, 20 women farmers immediately adopted SRI as a farming method under Pinky's guidance and met with considerable success. So far, 50 farmers in Pinky's VO have adopted the SRI and 35 members have kitchen gardens in their homes. The early adopters were also 'rewarded' with a rechargeable torch.

With Jeevika's current focus on nurturing community producer groups, Pinky's VO members have also attended video screenings on mushroom cultivation and poultry farming. There has been a palpable acceptance of the mushroom cultivation technique in Nahub and a positive reception of the improved and cost-effective techniques to boost productivity. 'Jeevika has mobilized housewives like me to find a voice and become change agents,' says Pinky.

Four months ago, Digital Green introduced a participatory learning approach for farmers in Pinky's area. The NGO encourages farmers to produce and share videos that demonstrate innovative agricultural practices; thereby empowering communities to learn from each other.

Pinky says, 'I feature in videos where I explain the best practices and I watch similar productions of other farmers. This way I don't have to visit individual farmers to disseminate information. Moreover, the camera and projector are easy to use and make for an incredible experience. With this technology, I aim to include 70-80 farmers in our SRI fold by 2014.'

'We women have our own identity now. Today, men ask us to pave the way for them to follow,' she beams with confidence.

Saberaben A. Ghanchi

Sky's the limit

Secretary, District Association and Member, SEWA Executive Committee

If you happen to come across this ordinary looking woman in the Gujarati-style sari, you might not give her a second glance. However, you will surely pay attention when she whips out her mobile phone and begins to recite rapid-fire orders for rice, spices, and jaggery. This intriguing mix of technology and tradition is Saberaben Ghanchi.

Saberaben was extremely lucky to have two people in her life who encouraged her to make something of herself beyond household drudgery and occasional stints as a daily wage worker – her mother and her husband. 'The daily-wage work allotted to me was very far from home, and I used to return very late at night. My in-laws used to get angry, but my husband said that I should carry on with my work.'

Sabera grew up in an impoverished home – the fact that she was allowed to study till grade ten was unusual given her circumstances. She was married at the relatively late age of 17. Her husband worked in a factory and brought home only 1500 rupees, hardly enough for two meals a day for a family of 6. 'In order to add to his income, I used to do stitching work and small jobs. Then one day, Parvinben from SEWA came on her rounds, telling us about savings schemes. I immediately asked her if I could join, as I desperately needed some work and an income.'

That was 2001. Today, Saberaben works with the district association as a Secretary, and is also a member of the Executive Committee of SEWA. She started off as a co-ordinator for the welfare of women widowed during the Godhra riots, getting them employment, and an education for their children. She formed associations and saving groups in her own village, helping the villagers get loans. One of her more memorable projects was with beedi-rollers, helping them acquire identity cards. For this, she had to stay in another village for days, a highly unusual thing for a rural woman to do.

Now Saberaben is a part of the agrarian products processing and marketing network of SEWA, RUDI. 'I used to go door-to-door in villages to market RUDI products. Now, things have changed – customers come and place orders with me. I also get orders for rice, spices etc for marriages, temple functions, and tea stalls.' She encourages other women to join RUDI and participate in its income generating activities.

But the most exciting experience for Saberaben has been RUDI Sandesha Vyavahar. Every Rudiben (member of RUDI) is given a mobile phone, and also trained in its use to help her with her work. Sabera goes to villages and collects orders for commodities, and then for just a rupee, she sends an SMS to the Ahmedabad headquarters, where the orders are kept ready for delivery. 'With the use of technology in the form of RUDI Sandesha Vyavhar, I'm able to reduce my cost of commuting and also save a fair amount of time to increase my sales. My income has increased from around 1,700 rupees to 5,000 rupees.'

Sabera has seen to it that her children are all well-educated. 'I've taken a bank loan for my elder son to start his business.' Her daughter has graduated with a B.Com and an LLB. She says, 'I'm also contributing to repaying our home loan, and my other income pays household expenses. I have become the owner and manager of my work and feel proud of it. I have become a dignified member of my society.'

રૂડી
RUDI
એગમાર્ક
ધાણાજીરૂ પાવડર

Meera H. Sanyal

Corporate mogul with a heart

President, Liberals India for Good Governance; Former CEO and Chairperson, Royal Bank of Scotland, India

During the 26/11 terrorist attacks on Mumbai in 2009, a senior banker and my mentor was murdered. This was a major turning point in my life. As the shock of the attacks faded, it was clear that without competent and effective political leadership, every aspect of our lives were at stake. However, I felt that simply criticizing the system and taking part in candlelight marches was not the solution. It was important to take a stand and engage constructively with the democratic process. Therefore in 2009, I stood to be elected into the Lok Sabha as an Independent candidate from South Mumbai. At the time, my actions were considered quixotic by many. I lost those elections, but learnt a great deal about my city and the hearts of its people. This experience also helped me embark on a new journey.

I don't belong to a political family. My father, a naval officer and a deeply idealistic person, brought us up to love India, and imbued in us his belief that each of us must serve our country. He led by example working for the Navy till the day he died. My mother, a lawyer, gave up her legal practice to be a full time wife and mother. From her, my brother and I learnt about the practical aspects of life; that no job was too small but also that no dream was too big. My husband Ashish, has always been a wonderful partner and friend.

I was fortunate to have the opportunity to study at some of the finest educational institutions in India and abroad. I started my banking career 30 years ago with Grindlays Bank. I have been fortunate to work with organisations like Lazards, ABN AMRO, and RBS, which gave me the opportunity to explore different facets of banking. In many ways, I became an 'Intrapreneur' in these organisations and looking back, feel happiness and pride in the new teams, projects, and companies that I was able to establish.

In 2001, I had the opportunity to set up ACES, the global offshore services entity for RBS (then ABN AMRO) in India – which grew from a small team of 6 persons to an organization that provided careers for over 21,000 young people. As mentor of the bank's microfinance program, I was able to play a part in financing over 6,50,000 women entrepreneurs across India. We then took this a step further and provided skill-based training and grants in the form of seed capital to 75,000 women in tribal and forest areas, helping them become proudly self-sufficient solo-preneurs (solo entrepreneurs)!

In March 2013, I made the decision to relinquish my post as CEO of RBS India, in order to devote time to the economic, social, and political causes that I am passionate about. By the end of December 2013, I will step down from my role as Chairperson of RBS – and will stand for the 2014 Parliamentary elections once again.

Of late, I have been delighted to see a rising wave of independent citizen candidates and newly formed political parties. It is as if the floodgates have opened, and the common citizen has said 'Enough'. The initial reluctance to participate in politics has given way to the realization that politics do matter. We can no longer abdicate the space of governance of our nation to people we don't respect or trust. We can and must participate not just in the political debate, but in the process itself. We all have a story, which often starts with one small step. In 2009, I took my first step.

Sister Mariola

An activist nun

State Coordinator, Prison Ministry India

'Being unwanted, unloved, uncared for, forgotten by everybody, I think that is a much greater hunger, a much greater poverty than the person who has nothing to eat' – thus spoke Mother Teresa. And so discovered an English teacher, Sister Mariola Sequeira when she yielded to the soft unknown voices across the wall from Sophia College in Ajmer, Rajasthan.

Her curiosity about a 'whole population' on the other side of the college finally compelled her to visit the imposing fort-like edifice, the Ajmer Central Jail. 'I didn't know what to expect, but I knew that I wanted to do something related to the prison,' she says. Some interactions later, she found out that several women inmates were in serious danger of being forgotten under sentences longer than the law required. Others were on indefinite wait-lists pending for their trials. She says, 'Talking to them, I realized there was a lot of frustration and isolation. It was most heart-wrenching to see that the women were out of touch with their children and families.'

When Sister Mariola embraced the religious congregation of the Mission Sister of Ajmer in 1979, she chose a consecrated life 'to be lived for the people, helping them, no matter if it is recognized or not'. Although her path to her purpose was broadly outlined, the women in Ajmer Jail clarified her role.

It was Bimla, an inmate, whose despondent plight spurred Sister Mariola to action. Accused of murdering her daughter-in-law, Bimla was languishing in jail, serving an 18-year-long sentence. Sister Mariola dug deeper, met Bimla's family in the village and deduced that the daughter-in-law had in fact, committed suicide. Sister Mariola persuaded Bimla's lawyer to appeal to the court with new evidences. Six arduous years of persistence later, the court acquitted Bimla and Mariola enabled her to reunite with her grandchildren. 'Each time, it's the poor who are the casualties. They are just shoved into prisons,' says Mariola.

There was more to the pathetic lives of the women inmates. They were engulfed by an emptiness that was a by-product of being disconnected from their families and with unbearable time on their hands. Mariola taught them, among other things, to make paper bags from newspapers and now helps sell their hand-made items. From legal intervention to rehabilitation, Mariola provided hope to the 'thrice discriminated; on account of being women, illiterate and without legal aid. If there's any group in this prison that deserves my service, it is the women.'

In 2004, the Rajasthan Government appointed Mariola as a member of state's Minority Commission in recognition of her service and advocacy for women under trials. She remains an active member of the People's Union for Civil Liberties (PUCL) Rajasthan, the state coordinator of the Prison Ministry India (PMI), and an NGO member of the Grievance Committee on Sexual Harassment at the Workplace at Central Jail, Ajmer. She emphasizes, 'My work is not just scratching the surface to get legal help for those under trial. I'm working for policy changes.'

In March 2010, television news channel CNN-IBN awarded Sister Mariola the Real Heroes Award for her work in rehabilitating women prisoners. She, in turn, dedicated the award to 'the unfortunate people in prisons'. Mariola continues to lobby for open prisons and prisoners' rights to enable them to 'live like normal human beings'. Sister Mariola Sequeira is a 'real hero': compassionate, benevolent, humanitarian, woman.

Sunita Kasera

Through her lens

Fearless Scribe

Sunita Kasera, an unassuming woman from Karauli, Rajasthan has been challenged, threatened and harassed by the people that she wants to pull-up, question, and expose. She is the only female committee member of the local district journalists' association, Video Volunteers. Sunita represents a less than minority group of rural women in Rajasthan: she is a graduate. Sunita, now a mother of three, wanted to pursue her education but her family decided to get her married. 'A few days after my wedding, I learnt that my new family was in the throes of a financial crisis. I secretly began sewing clothes to sell. I was able to ease the pain with my earnings,' she says.

Sunita's contribution and progressive attitude was a bold move in a deeply patriarchal society. In her spare time, Sunita joined Sathya Naval Development, an NGO that helps provide rural communities in Rajasthan access to basic human rights. It was here in 2010 that she became acquainted with India Unheard, the first community news service that wanted to create a 'network of community correspondents to tell unique stories; stories about their own communities; stories which are otherwise left untold', focusing on poverty, injustice and inequality. She signed up for the job, a paying one, and was selected to train in video journalism.

Equipped with critical thinking skills from her training, armed with a camera, and encouraged by her husband, Sunita set out to encapsulate the travails of women and children in Rajasthan. 'The most important part of my work is to create videos and bring about change. Through video activism, I enabled 20 women to receive funds due to them from the government. These women brewed illegal liquor for a living. Under the substitute employment scheme, they were taught a new skill set: tailoring. Following their training, these women were meant to receive 30,000 rupees and a sewing machine for their own start-ups. All kinds of bureaucratic delays stalled their payments. I made a video on their struggle, showed it to the social welfare authorities and followed it through over two months. The officer in-charge harassed me through the investigation but eventually the monies were released. I was present for the occasion when the women received their cheques. Their joy reaffirmed my faith in my mission,' she says.

When Sunita heard about the Kishori Balika Yojna for young girls, she found that the teens in her community were unaware of the scheme. She dug deeper and found that girls were entitled to receive free iron tablets but the Anganwadi, the government-run pre-school responsible for its dispersal, had no means to reach these girls. Sunita shot a video and made the girls watch it to learn about the benefits of the iron supplement tablets. 'Now the girls go to the Anganwadi to collect them,' she says. Sunita also took up the cause of artisans of the unorganized lacquer industry and the health risks they faced. She has also captured on film the life of the Gadiyanwal tribe who live out of a cart. Her work aims to draw attention to this alternative way of living, while at the same time portraying the people in a dignified manner. Sunita has reported on the lack of public toilets in the Karauli market and its impact on public health. 'I don't fear anybody. I can go anywhere to film whatever I need to for my reports,' she declares confidently.

'Ever since I have become a community correspondent, people treat me with respect. I have been recognized and appreciated for my hard work in this field and I want to continue doing so.' Sunita Kasera has a voice and she has made it heard and seen!

The **Healers**

'The best way to find yourself is to lose yourself in the service of others.'

Mahatma Gandhi

Asma Rahim

Medicine for the masses

Public Health Professional

It is difficult to encapsulate Dr. Asma Rahim in a few short paragraphs. Her achievements are numerous – from being one of the region's most prolific community medicine and public health experts, to writing a clear and practical textbook: *Principles and Practice of Community Medicine* that thousands of students are grateful for, and her research into rheumatology along with her several awards, fellowships, and accolades.

Most of all, though, what is admirable is her attitude. Born into a conservative yet educated Muslim home in Kozhikode, Asma's father was a doctor, and she and her sister were actively encouraged to follow in his footsteps. Asma graduated in medicine from Kasturba Medical College, Mangalore, and went on to do a medical degree in Community Medicine. Her choice of subject was a matter of great controversy within her family. 'Everyone wanted me to become a gynecologist. Female physicians, surgeons, and public health professionals were very rare those days. I had to face a lot of questions. But I wanted to do something different. I wanted to work among the public to promote awareness on preventing diseases and promoting health.'

Currently, Asma is an Additional Professor in the Department of Community Medicine, as well as the Convener of the Medical Council of India's Regional Centre for Medical Education at her alma mater in Kozhikode. They conduct workshops for over 200 teachers across 14 schools in South India on contemporary teaching and learning methods every year. 'Medical teaching is the only field where teachers are not given formal training. I am proud to be a teacher of teachers.'

Though Asma has been lauded for her internationally published research papers, which she has presented at conferences in India and abroad, her greatest sense of achievement comes from her community-based projects. 'We identified and trained women in the local Self Help Groups (SHGs), some of them with only eight to ten years of schooling, to identify fevers like chikungunya and dengue early, thus preventing complications and saving lives.' Appreciation from the urban and rural communities has helped boost her morale. Asma has been married for 24 years to a pediatrician, who she says is her 'greatest supporter, critic and soulmate'. However, one of Asma's toughest challenges was her very early marriage, which was forced on her right in the middle of her final year. 'I was dead against getting married that early, knowing fully well that I would be unable to cope with the demands of academics, family, and long-distance relationships. But all my pleading fell on deaf ears. It took almost seven to ten years for both of us to get settled, bring romance into our marriage, and to really get to know each other as individuals.'

Asma recognizes the challenge of balancing the professional and the personal for women. 'I am jealous of my male colleagues who have all the time to think about new ideas, attend meetings and seminars, write articles outside the working hours. I think for a woman who wants to have the best of both worlds, one should learn the art of making meaningful choices. When we decided to have a second child, I took a sabbatical and spent a year as a full-time mom. But my work never suffered since I started working on my textbook at the time!' Asma has no plans to stop now. She has just completed an International Fellowship in Medical Education from the PSG Regional Institute, Coimbatore. 'I would love to be a student all my life,' she says. 'In my old age, god willing, if I look back, I would love to be appreciated for the wonderful human being I was, rather than the academic accolades and the positions I have had.'

Chingutai Jadhav

Community comes first

Village Do-Gooder

Stories about empowered women are touching and inspiring. Not just because their principal characters have been powerless, oppressed, and browbeaten but more so because they spring from their contretemps to create social change. Chingutai from Medsinga village in Osmanabad district is one such woman, and despite her prevailing challenges, she stays committed to the service of others.

Chingutai was 17 and barely educated when she was married off to a man who she says, 'Showed me no respect or affection.' Two years later, she gave birth to a baby girl even though her husband was involved with another woman. 'One day, my daughter went out with her father and he came back with a dead body,' says Chingutai choking with emotion. She returned to her parents who believed their son-in-law was responsible for their grand-daughter's death. 'The judicial system has prolonged my anguish for 10 years now, and the matter is yet to be resolved.'

It was in 1997 when Swayam Shikshan Prayog (SSP), an NGO dedicated to building and strengthening women's organizational capabilities through self-education, reached out to Chingutai. Its leaders persuaded her to join a Self Help Group (SHG) to help rebuild her confidence through interactions with other women. In six months, Chingutai bought a sewing machine and began tailoring on a small scale. It was a tiny first step towards self-reliance but a leap thereafter when she started teaching women how to sew. Other opportunities presented themselves to her. Chingutai actualized an SHG venture to sell vessels, spices, and flour, and managed to procure 50 per cent of the subsidized amount from the Women and Child Department. Her venture grew and so did its prospects with the purchase of spice and flour making machines.

One of her most outstanding contributions to her community was helping to rehabilitate village folk in the aftermath of a devastating earthquake. 'Some 70 families were left homeless like I was, and we rebuilt our homes on our agricultural land which lacked basic facilities. For 10 years thereafter, we had to purchase drinking water until I sought out the Block Sabhapati and got him to see our living conditions. A month later, all 70 families had access to a clean water supply.'

Chingutai went on to form a BPL (Below Poverty Line) group for women linked to the District Rural Development Agency which enabled her to receive a loan of 2.50 lakh rupees to rear goats. In 2005, eight years after her first endeavour, Chingutai assumed a leadership role and turned her attention towards raising health standards in the community. 'Our services were promoted by SSP, and I was able to enrol 150 families into our programme. We extended quality care in health emergencies in addition to providing preventive health education to the families,' she elaborates.

While Chingutai grieved over her personal loss and coped with the litigation process, she continued to expand her realm of work. She has talked local political leaders into building a community hall, distributed chlorine tablets to clean water, mobilized women to plant over 1000 saplings, created over a 100 kitchen gardens for vegetable farming and trained women's agricultural groups to grow organic cash crops. Chingutai is also committed to the children in her village. 'Every year I identify and adopt malnourished children and place them with Anganwadis (child-care centres). I want to serve the poor and I feel good when I do something good for my community. It is my dream to be like Rani Laxmi Bai of Jhansi and Sindhutai Sapkal, invincible and spirited.' Many will say that Chingutai is already living her dream!

DUREX

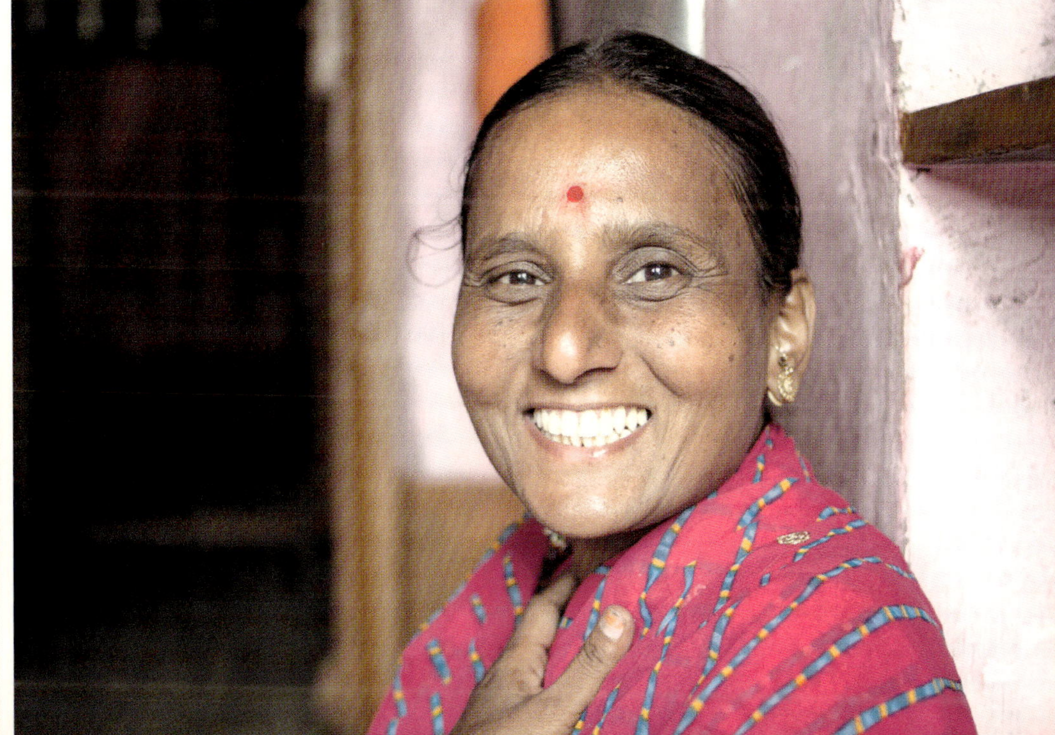

Fehmida Malik

Enabling the positive

Founder, Sambodh Charitable Trust

Fehmida Malik's understanding of empowerment comes from close encounters that might have scarred another person forever. Fehmida, however, channeled her experiences into a role so positive that she not only empowered herself, but also 2,000 women in the slum community of Vatva, Ahmedabad. 'Earlier, my sisters in the community never went out. They didn't even know who their neighbours were... now they go everywhere on their own, without any men. They went to represent us in Pune for a seminar!'

Armed with an MA in Clinical Psychology, Fehmida was all set to embark upon a career working with the mentally challenged. But destiny intervened in the form of the 2002 Gujarat riots. With horror, Fehmida watched the destruction unleashed against the Muslim people. She saw that those affected were the poorest. People lost their homes, their livelihoods, as well as their peace of mind. She began working with the children in the refugee camp at Vatva. Soon, she managed to garner some funding to improve the lives of the refugees through sanitation, nutrition, and health. However, rampant corruption among the NGOs she was associated with disillusioned her. She determined to start her own organization. And that is how the Sambodh Charitable Trust was born in 2004. Since she had been working with the community for a while, she managed to rustle up 47 volunteers and they began to find ways to make the lives of the slum dwellers more independent and sustainable.

First off, the task was to create a certain degree of economic empowerment. But how? Most of the men in the slum refused to let their wives even speak to Fehmida. Slowly, whittling away at the distrust, the volunteers managed to convince the women to start participating in the co-operative credit scheme they had set up in 2007, called Sarijan Mahila Credit Co-operative Society. 'Earlier women used to hide and give us their savings, now times have changed and men come and give us their wives' savings,' she says. The scheme allowed women to maintain a zero balance account and deposit as little as 50 rupees per month. 'The best thing is, from deposits of 50 rupees each month, we have now provided loans totaling up to 21 lakhs and the plus point is, we don't even have one defaulter.' The women can thus put aside money for emergencies, school fees and the like, as well as take loans.

Fehmida's philosophy is simply this: 'We feel that if people have savings, they start thinking about health and education... but if they have no savings, they cannot think of these things. Economic empowerment is thus very important. That is why for livelihood, we give a loan immediately, so that they can do business and their standard of living can improve.' Some of Fehmida's landmark work has been in health, natal care and government schemes. 'I have seen a change in the last 10 years. My sisters in the community now know how to deal with the government and how to ask for help.'

In Vatva, 2,000 women (out of a total population of 10,000) are part of Sambodh's programmes. Men are beneficiaries too, but 'only after the woman opens an account can her husband have one,' says Fehmida. Now that the organization is up and running, Fehmida's work has become more 'high-level'. She looks out for funding from the government and foreign agencies. (Sambodh was started with the help of the Indo-Global Social Service Society). 'My role is to help the 11 core members of the co-operative, to take them to a place where they can set up their own co-op, to train and motivate them, give them funding and exposure.' She credits her success to her family and her father, who gave her the strength to become who she is. This fabulous motivator has chosen to stay single and devote her life to the community.

Kanku Bai

550 babies to her name

Trained Midwife

When Kanku Bai was a girl, herding her parents' cattle along with her two sisters (while her brothers went to school), the future she imagined for herself was probably a good deal different from where she stands today. Kanku never went to school. She comes from a small village in Rajasthan. She was married off at 17.

Who would have thought then, that one day she would have delivered over 550 babies?

Kanku's life was no different from any other girl in rural India – running her home, serving her in-laws, looking after her husband and children's needs. She would occasionally assist the midwife in the village when a baby was being born. But fate had other plans for her. Seva Mandir, an NGO, holds Village Development Committee meetings in rural Rajasthan regularly. This time, the agenda was a training programme for traditional birth attendants. The committee, looking at her past experience, recommended that Kanku be chosen for the training.

Much against the wishes of her in-laws who saw no merit in her leaving the confines of the home, she started attending the week-long training sessions. She soon learned some important lessons about safe motherhood, pregnancy, childbirth and antenatal care.

'My husband accompanied me to some of these classes. Then he understood the value of my work,' she says proudly. He began to support her whole-heartedly. And once she started bringing home a salary, her family was on her side too. Kanku Bai's children, including her two daughters, are all educated.

Today, Kanku Bai looks back on her work with pride. She has spent years making the lives of women and children in her village healthier, safer, and better. 'I feel honoured that my work as a traditional birth attendant gives me an opportunity to help save the lives of both women and newborns.'

Her work has rendered her proficient in so many areas. In assisting in aseptic deliveries and other emergency obstetric procedures; building trust in modern medicine within the community; encouraging institutional deliveries by personally accompanying hesitant mothers to hospitals; and using the traditional knowledge of her community to strengthen medical procedures. 'The respect I have earned in my community has allowed me to motivate other mothers to care for their daughters.'

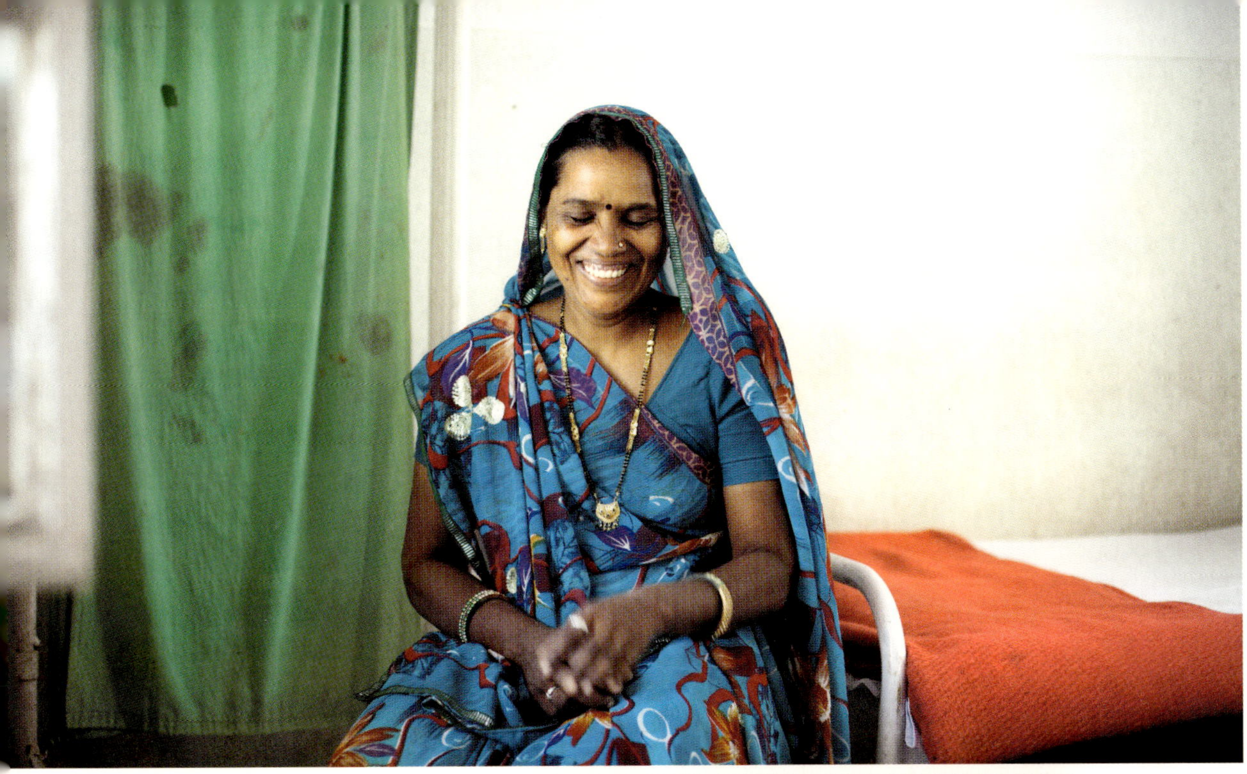

DISPO VAN
DISPO VAN

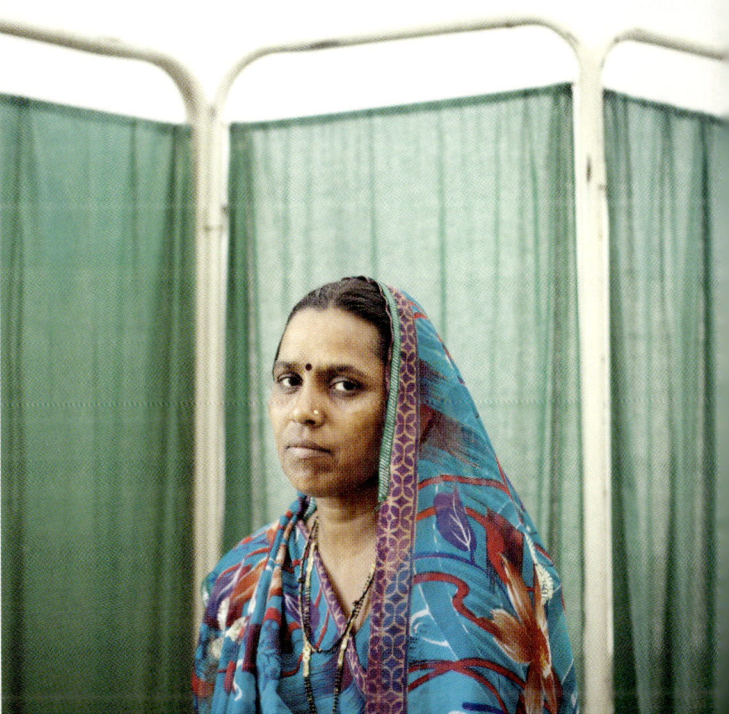

Indira Hinduja

Revising biology, rewriting history

IVF, Infertility Specialist and Gynecologist, P.D. Hinduja National Hospital and MRC.

Honorary Obstetrician and Gynecologist, Jaslok Hospital and Research Centre; Breach Candy Hospital Trust

The day started on a familiar note. I was in the midst of managing my daily OPD when I got a call requesting me to write a two-page account of my life. That set me thinking. I was born in Shikarpur in the erstwhile Sindh province (now Pakistan) as the youngest of eight children. Partition played an important role in my life as my parents had to move to India; and we found ourselves in Belgaum. My father ran a small business. I was sent to a Marathi-medium municipal school. The environment was unfavourable when it came to higher education for girls, but I wanted to continue with my studies in a private school. My family was supportive, and when I eventually gained admission into a bigger school, I became even more enthusiastic about higher education. The new school was an induction into a different culture and language. With consistent hard work, I managed to get into Nair Hospital and Topiwala National Medical college, in pursuit of a profession I was passionate about. It was my college library where I started enjoying reading – and that is how I kept myself updated with the latest research.

During my stint at KEM hospital as a Senior Registrar (after a few years at Nair Hospital), I was introduced to an interesting project at the Institute for Research in Reproduction in the Indian Council of Medical Research (ICMR). Dr. Peter of the institute was working on studies about 'reproduction in mice'. I started helping Dr. Peter and we tried to expand our studies to human beings, but to our disappointment, we were met with strong resistance from colleagues and seniors. Dr. Peter was soon compelled to resign from the institute, and I registered myself for a Ph.D.

My research was still in its primitive stage, with patients not being very forthcoming; I found it difficult to continue and under pressure from authorities, the dean of our college transferred me to Sion Hospital for a higher post – an offer I refused. I was debarred from any promotion at the medical institute for three years, thus leaving me with less salary. Those were difficult days as making ends meet became a serious concern. What kept me going during those trying days was my determination and hope. One generally tends to remember and be grateful to friends who help us through these tough periods, and for me, these friends were my books and my dreams.

It was now time for me to look for patients. I would stay for long hours in the OPD, counselling people. I contributed almost all of my salary towards their treatment without even thinking about my own basic needs. The initial period brought a lot of frustration with as many as 17 patients testing negative for pregnancy. With patient number 18, I tasted success, and as they say, the rest is history.

Without any doubt it is my mother and my dear friend and colleague, Dr. Kusum Zaveri, who have made the single largest impact on my life and provided me with motivation and a support system (emotional and monetary) when I needed it the most. Ultimately, Dr. Kusum Zaveri and I started our own IVF Centre – the Indira and Kusum Infertility Centre (INKUS).

The Government of India and Maharashtra have honoured me with many awards. It was my determination, honesty, and sincerity that made me what I am. When all these things come together, no force is strong enough to stop you. For all the years I struggled, hardships I faced, and odds I won against, I know that every time a patient smiles, I win.

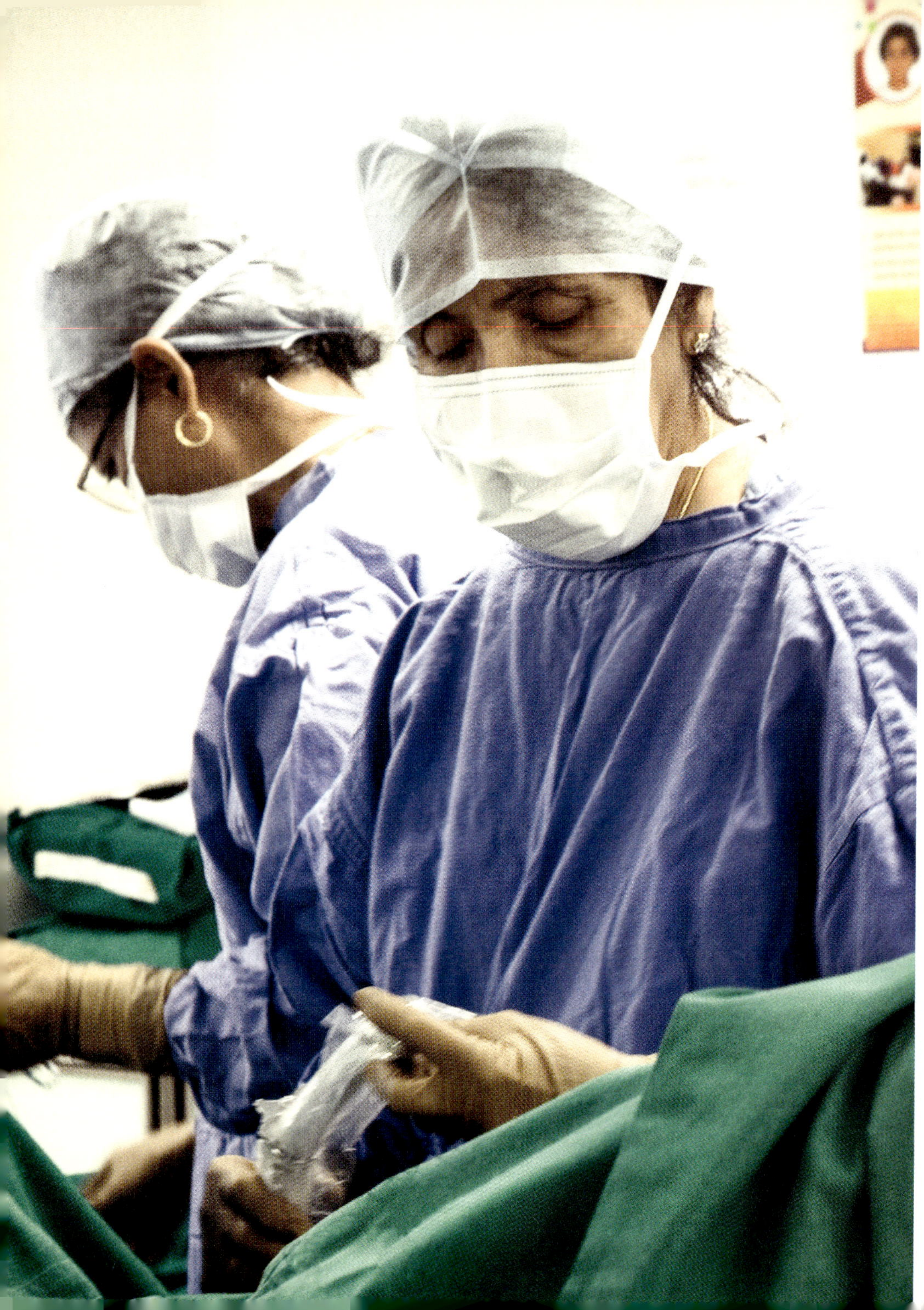

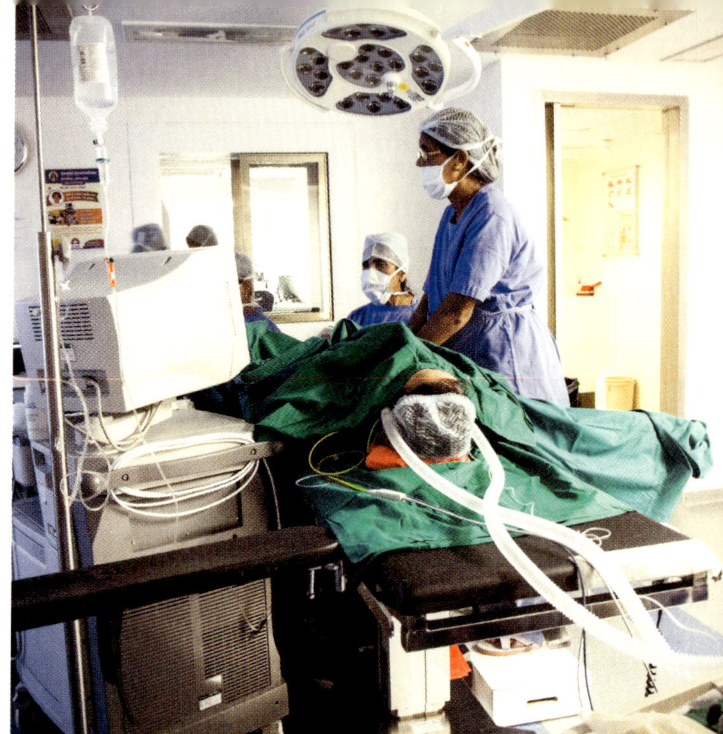

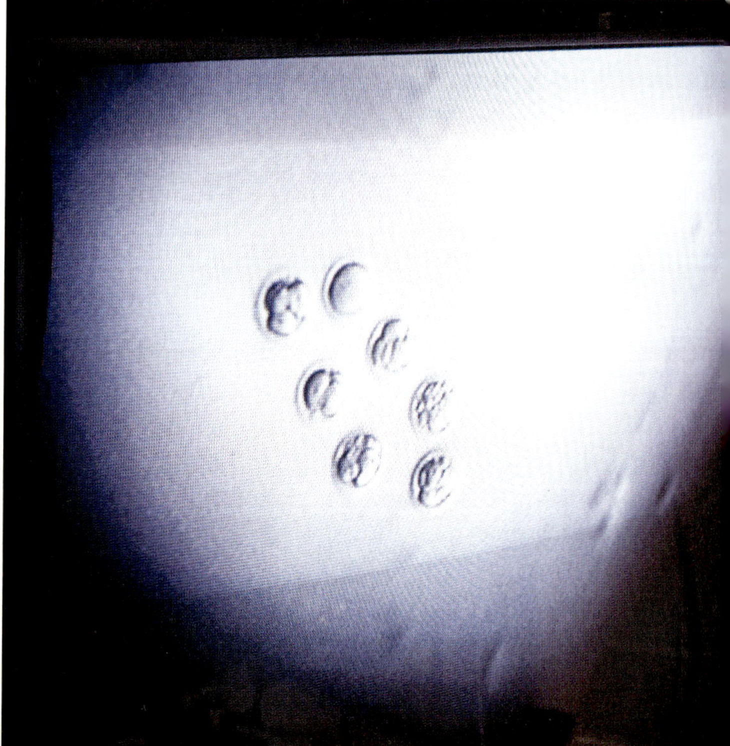

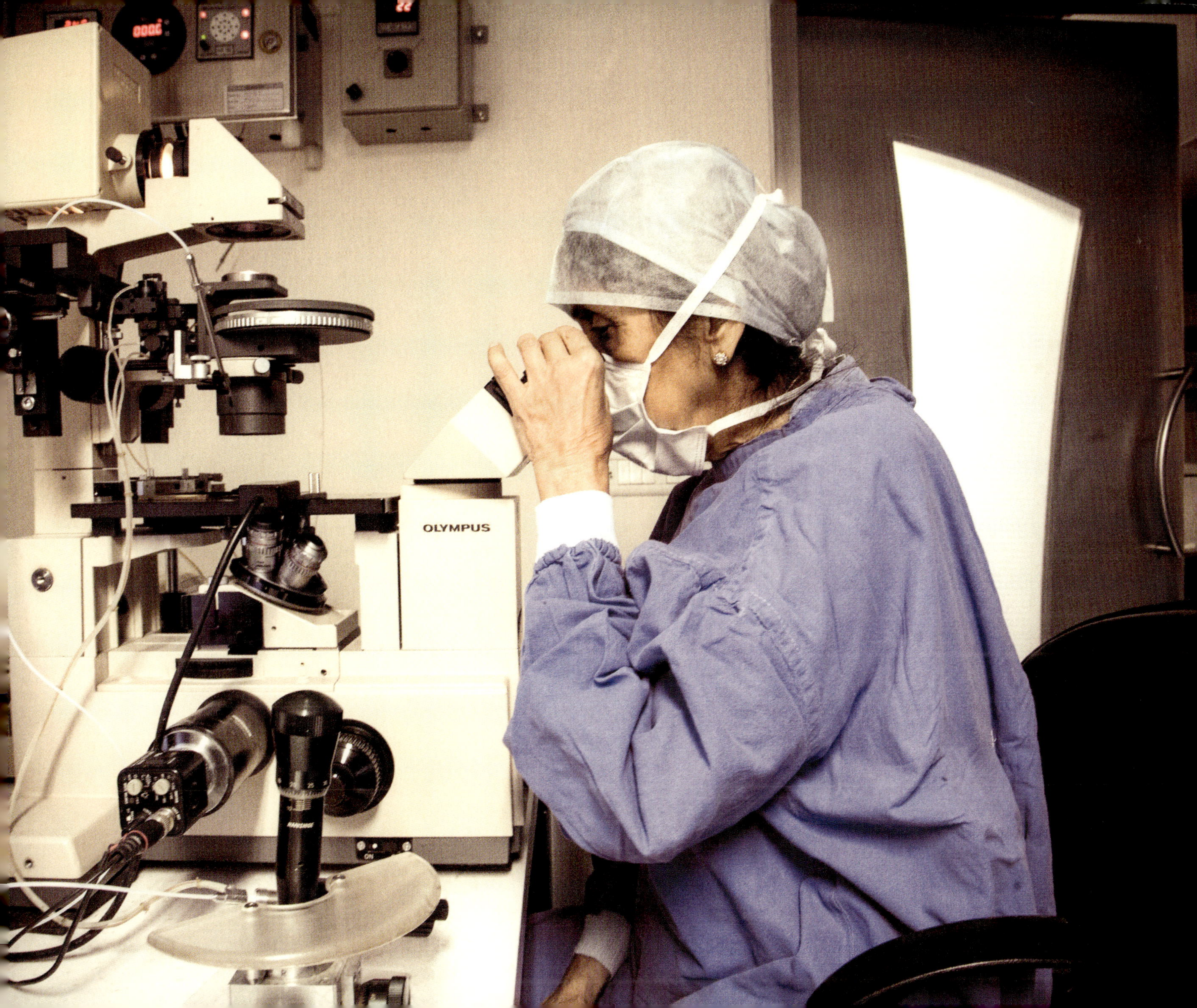
OLYMPUS

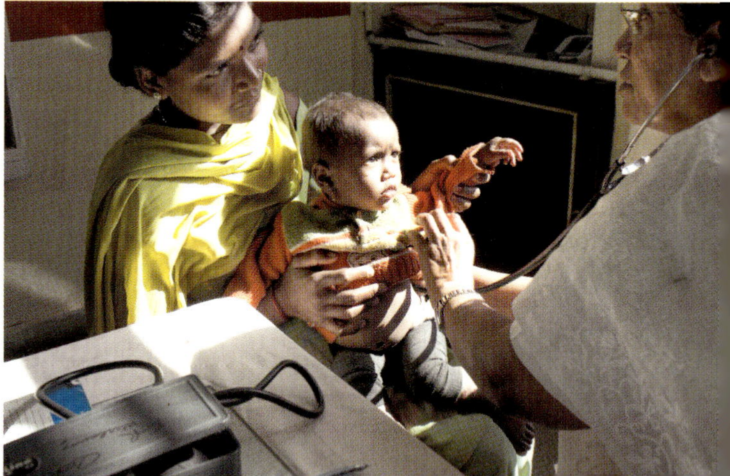

Kshama Metre

Self Help is the best help

National Director, CORD

Some say that the Hippocratic Oath is outdated with relevance to modern-day medicine. Yet, others who have held up their hand to it strive to expand the scope of the inspirational words. Dr. Kshama Metre took her oath when she earned her medical stripes with distinction and established a successful practice in Delhi. She was, by then, already deeply influenced by her upbringing and her father, who had instilled in her a deep desire to serve the community. She, however, was still searching for answers to her questions: who am I and what is life?

It was when Dr. Metre met Swami Chinmayananda (Guru*ji*) three decades ago, that she experienced a paradigm shift. 'Guruji asked me to take care of the people around Sidhbari, and my internal voice urged me to go about it, that's how I came to beautiful Himachal Pradesh,' she says. In 1985, Dr. Metre joined the Chinmaya Rural Primary Health Care and Training Centre at Sidhbari and set up the first maternal and child health services in the area. Back then, the underdeveloped state was plagued by illiteracy, poor living, and adverse health conditions. 'The villagers faced so much struggle that if I were to work only in health, I would just be touching the tip of the iceberg. I knew we had to address other issues that impacted their lives,' she reminisces.

Dr. Metre realigned her development initiatives to embrace the most underprivileged members of the community, the women. 'Women are definitely the core of the home. If they can manage a home, they can certainly manage a village. I ask the women to think of what would happen to India if they all went on a holiday for a day. That's how they realize their self-worth. They are definitely contributing to the economy,' she opines.

In 1987, Dr. Metre set up Mahila Mandals, a village-level forum for rural women to discuss and participate in personal and social, economic, environmental, educational, health, gender, and self-governance matters. For Dr. Metre, these Mandals and the societal concerns they highlighted burgeoned the need to create Chinmaya Organization for Rural Development (CORD) in the same year. As National Director of CORD, Dr. Metre strategized to further facilitate integrated and sustainable development in rural areas. She and her volunteers now support and address programmes on rural poverty, adult literacy, healthcare and nutrition, micro-banking and income generation, rehabilitation of children with disabilities, and natural resource management.

A pioneer of the early microfinance revolution in India, Dr. Metre's laudable efforts have enabled a 100 million people to gain access to financial credit. 'The self help movement is a microfinance movement and largely a women's operation wherein 20 women come together to improve their lives by learning to save, operate democratically, generate income, and keep records,' she says. 'One of the reasons for poverty in rural areas is low access to credit and finance services. While we have had nationalized banks since 1969, the services of the delivery model were not matched to the needs of the people. Now, more than 400 women join this movement every hour, an NGO joins every day, and 3.5 million new women become SHG members.' CORD now serves 27, 000 members spanning up to 900 villages.

Those are not the only impressive outcomes. Dr. Metre has an endless list of awards, including a Padma Shri. While Dr. Metre has honoured her oath and accepted her awards with humility, she believes her work isn't about her. 'The people themselves are most important actors in change,' she says.

Meeratai Umbre

Daughter of the soil

Farmer

In India the sex-ratio demographic crisis looms large and female foeticide is a horrifying reality. The United Nations now calls India the most dangerous place on earth for a girl. Meeratai Umbre, 30, is a stark exception to this enumeration as she grew up in a large family of 24 members, loved and adored.

Meeratai could not attend school beyond a primary level for lack of facilities in her village of Dindegaon in Tuljapur district in Maharashtra. At sixteen, she was wedded to Arun Umbre from the military service. 'My new family was a large one too and in our common resources we shared 45 acres of land. Some years later when the members separated we got only six acres in our share,' she says.

Deeply rooted in farming through her growing-up years, Meeratai attempted to grow grapes in an acre of her land. 'It was a successful venture for six years. In the seventh year, my vineyard was ravaged and destroyed by insects and pests. The timing of this huge loss coincided with my husband's retirement. All of a sudden, we were faced with extreme financial hardship and the continuing responsibility of educating our two sons,' she recalls.

In order to stabilize their resources, her husband took up a job as a security guard and Meeratai leased her land for a small annual income. Meanwhile, she joined an organization that worked with Self Help Groups (SHGs) to develop women's capacity building. Over the years, Meeratai became adept in her organizational skills and was identified by Naseem Sheikh and Godavari of Swayam Shikshan Prayog. They recognized Meeratai's farming experience and persuaded her to form a women's group to spotlight and encourage innovative agricultural practices. Meeratai and her group members took the plunge. She began by sending out samples of their farm soil to experts at the Krishi Vigyan Kendra (KVG) and with the feedback they received they would adjust the usage and quantity of organic manure.

With these new insights, Meeratai sought a loan and laid a 2,800 feet pipeline for irrigation from the nearby lake to her farm. The yield from her farm land increased manifold and Meeratai shared her valuable knowledge on organic farming with KVG and other farmers through her talks on All India Radio, Osmanabad. She has thus initiated an effective extended education through peer-to-peer communication.

Along the way, Meeratai bought two buffaloes and now earns 3,000 rupees from the sale of milk. A new venture calls for new learning and Meeratai continues to widen her knowledge base through attending animal husbandry workshops. She now plans to seek a loan to form a milk cooperative in her village.

From organic farming to dairying, Meeratai's journey towards self-reliance has made her an earning member of her family. For any committed social worker, the wheels of service do not halt at income generation. Meeratai offers counselling support to adolescent girls and HIV positive patients as an Accredited Social Health Activist (ASHA) even as she continues to constitute the formation of new SHGs. Her philosophy is simple: 'We must continue to work innovatively and the rest will fall into place.'

Meeratai is an exceptional woman and a true daughter of the soil.

Ranno Devi

Saved by an SMS

Proactive Mother

Heroism does not always lie in empowering others – often, empowering oneself is the hardest and most challenging task. Ranno Devi and her family live a life where survival is an everyday struggle.

With a salary of 4,000 rupees brought home by her husband from his temporary job at a nearby sweet shop, she somehow manages to feed her 10-year-old daughter and 1-month-old son. A tiny plot of land yields little wheat to meet the family's needs. Yet, when the daughter goes to school, she exhibits a certain desire for bettering their lives. A desire shared by all mothers when it comes to the growth, safety, and well being of their children, and their own reproductive health.

When an economically disadvantaged woman like Ranno gets pregnant, she relies on local midwives, or simply the vagaries of nature to deliver her child. Often blinded my superstitious misconceptions, such women often put their infant's (and not to mention their own) lives at risk. The weekly visit to the doctor, frequent scans, and healthy diet are non-existent. 'I could not afford the doctor's fee to get guidance for a safe delivery, as the state-run health services are very poor in our area,' she explained.

Then one day, a health motivator visited her house, and seeing that she was expecting a child, suggested that she register herself as a beneficiary in a unique scheme. This scheme uses the power of telecom technology to do a wonderful thing: it sends reproductive and child health information directly to her, as an SMS!

During the entire period, Ranno would receive two localized SMSs every week in Hindi which informed her about everything she needed to know about a safe and healthy pregnancy and nursing period. These messages are pre-determined, pre-vetted digital content as per government guidelines. They are also detailed, descriptive and medically accurate. Ranno is grateful for this. She says, 'I followed all the instructions, and gave birth to a healthy son after a normal delivery.' Besides pregnancy-related information, the women are also sent tips on nutrition, rest, and exercise. Even after the baby is born, there is a follow-up round of SMSs about ante-natal checkups, vaccines, supplements, the normal growth and movement of the baby, and the recovery of the mother's womb and body.

'I also want to thank our health motivator for visiting my house twice a week during my pregnancy,' she says gratefully. Now that her son is a little older, she has signed up for the child health care service, which operates in a similar manner. She still receives the text messages, but now, they are aimed at the safety, growth, and well being of her children.

Ranno chose to adapt herself, challenged regressive beliefs, and allowed technology to better her life. She opened herself to new ways of learning and thinking, without clinging to old conventions, something that even educated, urbanized people find difficult to do.

That's real empowerment!

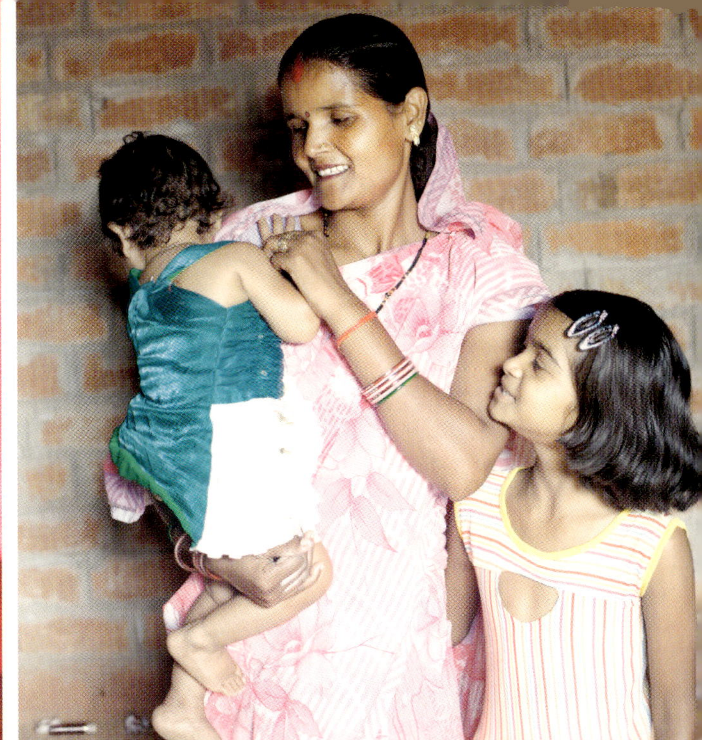

Renuka Dehatonde

Just positive

Helping AIDS Patients

Renuka's immunity was first threatened when her husband fell sick and was diagnosed HIV positive. The second blow came when he passed away due to his illness. The ground beneath her feet gave way when she was faced with her own truth. Renuka spiralled into despondency asking the one question that is uppermost in every HIV positive person's mind: Why me?

Growing up in a close-knit family is still a fond memory for Renuka. Her birth was a celebration for her parents who had longed for a child for seven years. Although her parents led a simple and meagre life, they ensured that Renuka went to school. So she did, and scored 72 per cent in the grade ten board examination, but her parents could not afford a higher education for her as they were obliged to school their three other children and care for some of their relatives. So, at 16, she was married off to Vishal, a musician. In a more financially secure home, Renuka learned to sew and went back to complete high school while tending to her home and in-laws. 'I enjoyed six years of blissful married life,' she says, 'but not for long.' Her husband took ill and was wrongly diagnosed with typhoid. Renuka says, 'His condition worsened and finally we went to the city of Ahmednagar to seek medical advice. Vishal's blood report revealed that he was HIV positive. I knew nothing about the disease or its consequences. His condition deteriorated rapidly and his death left me devastated.' As per the doctor's advice, Renuka got herself tested. 'My world collapsed when I found out I too was HIV positive. For me it was the beginning of my end,' recalls Renuka.

To add to her anguish and despair, her in-laws blamed her for their son's death. Confused, broken, embittered and in grief, Renuka questioned her existence. 'I believed I had no reason to live. My parents were as broken as I was and sent my brother to bring me back home. Their love and support gave me hope and helped me gather courage to face life.'

A month later, Renuka's father learned of the Snehlaya Community Care Centre (CCC) in Ahmednagar and took her there. She underwent Antiretroviral Therapy (ART) under the compassionate care of the medical staff. Renuka says, 'The environment was so comforting that I never felt lonely through my treatment. When it was time for me to leave I plunged into despair yet again dreading the thought of facing the world as a widow and HIV-positive person.' Snehalaya offered her the opportunity to stay at their centre and absorbed her in their Snehadhar project. Over four years, Renuka showed grit and perseverance as she dealt with her emotional issues. She cooked and cleaned at the centre and her sincerity and dedication got noticed. The management enrolled her at Ummeed's Child Development Centre and Tata Institute of Social Studies Child Development Aide (CDA) Programme. Renuka was appointed as a teacher at the newly opened Early Intervention Centre at Snehalaya to work with children of HIV positive parents and sex-workers.

Renuka works with a professional approach towards child development and care with underprivileged children who would otherwise have had little opportunity for formal schooling. She believes that her training enables her to give back to the community and has given her an opportunity to rebuild her life. 'This is the story of my journey from being a helpless HIV positive patient to becoming a responsible care-giver and teacher: helping others, giving and getting support and contributing to a community,' says Renuka. She survived through HIV and emerged stronger than ever.

Dr. (Capt.) Ritu Rajkishore Biyani

Driver. Driving. Driven

Founder, High>>>ways... Infinite Beyond Cancer

A disease so dreaded to most people that they dare not utter its name. But many cancer survivors explicitly reconstruct and share their ordeal in order to spread awareness. Ritu Biyani, 53, is a cancer survivor who did exactly that in her own unique and adventurous way.

Ritu served as a Captain in the Indian Army from 1981 until 1992. Three years into her service in 1984, she earned the distinction of becoming the first Lady Paratrooper of the Army Dental Corp. Through her stellar career, Ritu sought personal challenges through the thrills of skydiving, mountaineering, skiing, and trekking. In 2000, at the age of 40, Ritu processed emotionally shattering news when she was diagnosed with breast cancer. At that time her only child, Ms. Tista Joseph, was all of eight years old. While coping with her overwhelming diagnosis, Ritu experienced anxiety thinking about her daughter's future. So she decided to take the disease head on and give her survival a fighting chance.

Over the next five years Ritu underwent three surgeries and six cycles of chemotherapy. She braved this period with gumption and the attitude of an adventure enthusiast. As she began her healing and recovery process, Ritu realized that most individuals were clueless about the disease and its symptoms, and therefore ill-equipped to nip it in the bud. She resolved to link adventure sports with a cancer awareness mission across the country. It was a novel idea and also first of its kind in the country. In 2006, Ritu along with her teenage daughter Tista conceptualized and pioneered Project High>>>ways... and outlined three goals for her mission. First, to drive to the four tips of India, cross all the highest motorable roads, including the two of the world's highest road passes. Second, to conduct awareness camps and dispel myths, stigmas, ignorance, and fears using visual aids on breast, cervical, and oral cancers for people in near and far-flung areas. Third, to motivate cancer patients and survivors. Ritu says, 'My ultimate vision is to help reduce the occurence of advance cases through early detection. I want to make knowledge, resources, and expertise available in remote, rural, and urban areas. I want to instill hope in all those people who were touched by Cancer to celebrate health and life.' So Ritu got behind the wheel and Tista took charge as navigator and together they traversed over 30,220 kms in 177 days, touching the four tips of India at Kutch, Kanyakumari, Ladakh, and Arunachal Pradesh. This feat earned them a place in the 2007 and 2008 Limca Book of Records, India. En route, the duo spread awareness amidst people on symptoms, risk factors, preventive and protective lifestyles, importance of early detection, supportive care, and survivorship. 'The adventure was meant to inculcate an attitude to explore one's own inner strengths and spirits, unlock and expand one's horizons, steer through all odds, overcome the fear of the unknown in one's roller-coaster quest, celebrate one's existence and to experience those exhilarating moments of going beyond... all on the highway called life.' In 2008, she founded High>>>ways... Infinite Beyond Cancer. Through her initiative, she has empowered more than 1,78,000 people, provided supportive care to over 5,000 cancer patients, and driven solo over 1,00,000 kms.

Ritu has received accolades from tribal and village heads, organizations, the Armed Forces, and more. She has spoken at prestigious International Cancer Conferences, Cancer hospitals like TATA Memorial, corporates, educational institutions etc. She has received the Cancer Aid & Research Foundation (CARF) award for Outstanding Contribution in the Field of Cancer, and the Manthan Award South Asia for e-health, among others.

High>>>Ways...
Infinite

AN ADVENTURE WITH A VISION
Across the Country
Solo Drive
FORD ENDEAVOUR SUPPORTS
Project HIGH>>>WAYS
A BREAST CANCER AWARENESS PROGRAM
www.india.ford.com

It all began with
My Adventure with
Breast Cancer
in Sept 2000.
Simply by changing
gears incredible
journey on my own
High>>>ways...
beyond cancer

MS-CIT
Computing Essentials
PROGRAMME REVIEW AND STRATEGY DEVELOPMENT, INDIA

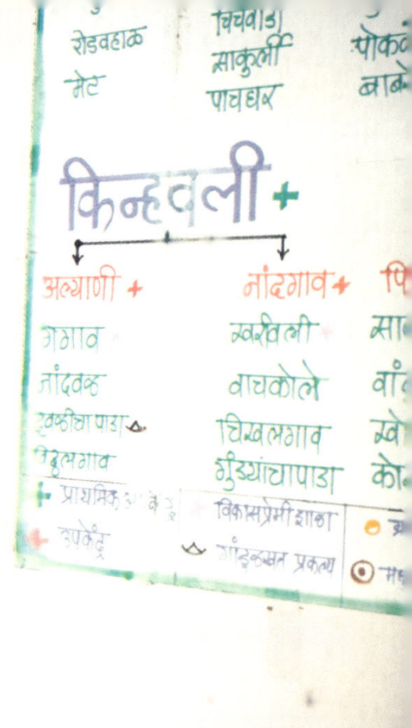
किन्हवली
अल्याणी
नांदगाव

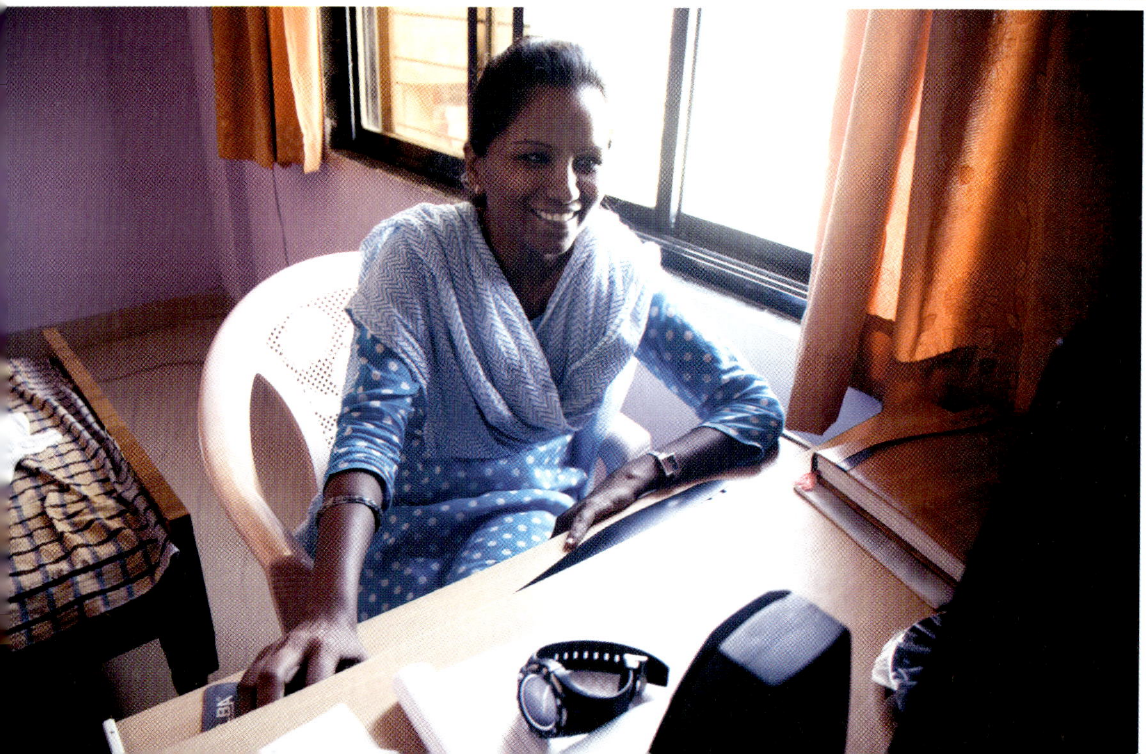

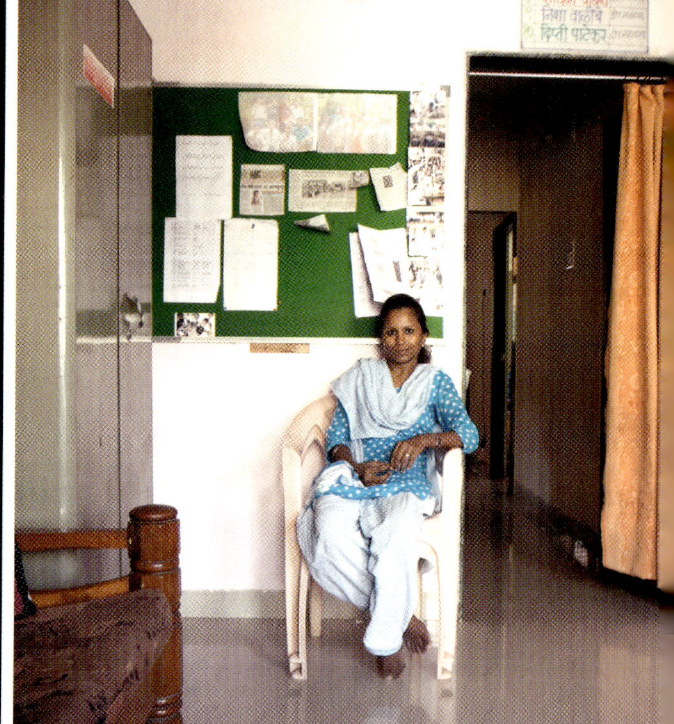

Sangita Tribhuvan

Motivator

UNICEF trained Social Worker

The little girl is scrubbing dishes. She still has to sweep the kitchen and soak *channa* for tomorrow's lunch and only after that can she start her homework. And then, before she leaves for school early the next morning, she will have to pack her uncle and cousins' lunch boxes. If this seems like a sad, cruel situation to you, think again. For Sangita Tribhuvan, it was a lifeline, a small price to pay for getting an education. When she was in grade five, Sangita was sent to her uncle's house in the city. Her uncle paid for her books and uniforms, and in return, she did household chores and babysitting duties. 'Our village school was only till the fourth grade. After that, if you wanted to continue, you had to travel 6 kms. Most of the girls dropped out of school right then. But not I.'

When she finished the twelfth grade, though, her uncle's business failed, and he could not sponsor her education any more. Sangita started looking for work. UNICEF had started some programmes in her village for girls and children. Sangita looked into these... and she knew she had found her calling.

She remembers, 'I used to see the women in my village who went to work in the neighbouring fields. Also, she and the other women expected their daughters to drop out of school, and accompany them. If it wasn't for my father, who insisted I study till at least the tenth grade, I would have met that same fate. I felt I had to do something about this – the state of women around me.' Her first project with UNICEF was to train school children in sanitation and personal hygiene. Since then, starting with small projects (which she also used to fund her bachelor's degree), she has steadily shouldered more responsibility, becoming a master trainer under UNICEF, leading and facilitating training for government workers, youth, and women.

Now, 34, Sangita works on issues ranging from sexual health and reproduction, education, the granting of basic rights like water and sanitation, safe motherhood, and income generation for rural women. She provides training, conducts workshops, and motivates people to fight for justice through collective action. For instance, in her village and others around, she has motivated women to come together and write to the Gram Panchayat and file police complaints to close down liquor shops in the area. 'The men spend money on alcohol, then cause trouble at home. They don't even spare the kids' school fees. We worked with the women to get the shops shut legally.'

She travels across nearly 70 villages in Thane district, spreading her message with conviction. Closest to her heart, however, are the projects that deal with adolescent girls. 'Girls drop out for the slightest of reasons. What I tell them is, show your parents you can do something different!' She uses her own example to illustrate. 'My parents fully support me. I think it is because I earn and provide for them. I bought a house in the village. I have helped my siblings get settled. People in the village look at me in wonder.'

The financial and emotional support she lends to her friends and family also allows her to live life on her own terms. She has told them firmly that she will only marry someone who respects her and accepts her for who she is. 'Every time a proposal would come, it would fall through because either they thought I was too educated; or they wanted me to give up my job and stay at home. I have worked hard for 12 years and reached somewhere. I'm not going to give it all up so easily!

The **Safekeepers**

'...for women are not only
the deities of the household fire,
but the flame of the soul itself.'

Rabindranath Tagore

Bimla Devi

Limitless

Worker, Sanjivani

When the right to public transport, to equal opportunity, to education, and to vote is denied to a person over and over again, any one of two things can happen. The person can waste away, becoming a helpless, disenfranchised mass of low self-esteem. Or the person can become Bimla Devi. Perhaps it was because as a poor dalit girl, she was discriminated against in every sphere of life; or maybe it was because she was often denied access to basic civic amenities; and not to forget how she was forced to drop out of school in grade eight (and was married off three years later); or it could just be because she is a remarkable personality – Bimla Devi became a fighter for the downtrodden.

'I was always good at my studies and wanted to become something. But given my situation, I decided to do whatever little I could, and help other women by making them aware and empowered. 'She started by gathering the women in her village together for regular *kirtan* (prayer) sessions at her house. During these sessions, she began to talk to them about their health, slowly getting them to open up without embarrassment about reproductive and sexual problems. Initially, the women resisted, but they soon realized the benefits this information would bring them. Bimla led by example: she chose to breastfeed her second child as she had been advised by the auxiliary nurse midwife. This dispelled the superstition in the village that women should not breastfeed their newborn children for three days after birth. 500 dalit women followed her example, and several took her advice to consult the ANWs for safe pregnancies and deliveries.

Next, she started introducing subjects like how crucial it was for them to exercise their right to vote. Conquering her own fears and ignoring the ridicule meted out by her peers, she attended a training session about Panchayati Raj in the neighbouring village, and began to pass on the newly-acquired information to the women in her group as well as the men. She explained to them how economic empowerment could change their lives. She began talking about gender equality too.

Her husband's family tried to stop her from leaving the house – they beat her, threatened her – but she held her own, with her husband's staunch support. 'They wanted me to be confined to the house. But I said no, I will go out, I will do my work. I will try to help others. If you can find that I am doing anything wrong, I will come back myself!' She finally had to resort to filing an FIR against them to be left in peace. Not one to allow any injustice to go unchallenged, Bimla Devi began to question the age-old practice perpetuated by the upper castes: of not allowing those of lower castes access to drinking water taps in her village. Her protests bore fruit – today, the drinking water tap is accessible to Thakurs and dalits alike.

She now works with the Haryana government through their NGO, Sanjivani. Her original work in reproductive health was so successful, that it needed to be taken to a higher level. This led to a unique project, where Bimla Devi would write a series of books to be distributed among other communities about healthy motherhood and reproductive well-being. Bimla Devi's work with the NGO comprises educating young girls of both upper and lower castes about gender, health, and discrimination. She also supports women who have been subjected to abuse through violence in the home, dowry demands, or female foeticide. She is the head of the Mahila Shakti Parishad in her area, as well as the chief of the Rewari District 4th Block Kisaan Union, through which she helps farmers fight for land rights and fair pricing. She says with a beaming smile, 'I am happy to be born a woman.'

Laxmi Lokhande

A clean sweep

Maker of Brooms and Ropes

Laxmi Lokhande remembers that she was married off around the time she began losing her baby teeth. Over the years her alcoholic husband stopped working and tending to the children and their lives slipped into abject poverty, living under a shelter made from straw. No longer able to cope with her husband's wastrel life, Laxmi took charge of their dwindling finances. She knew little beyond child-rearing and household chores though there was one skill she had acquired through heredity and tradition: broom making.

Laxmi capitalized on her skill and began to manually process wood fibres from trees in order to weave them into thread to make brooms and ropes. Her earnings were small, but Laxmi managed to open a savings account at a local bank in Mhaswad. Fortunately for her, the bank's primary objective and mission was to provide women in poverty-stricken Maharashtra with the tools to achieve financial independence and self-sufficiency. This, the bank offered through a unique and innovative combination of financial and non-financial services.

Laxmi also became a beneficiary of the financial literacy programme offered by the bank and attended classes offered by them to better understand the judicious use of money and this greatly contributed to her self-confidence too. She learned to spend less and save more. Following her training she became eligible to take small loans to procure raw materials till her business cycle stabilized.

As her sales picked up, Laxmi was able to get bigger loans at lower interest rates to further finance her thriving business. Laxmi's outstanding reputation and credibility in the market and amongst her customers boosted her business allowing her to make profits and single-handedly support her family.

Laxmi now nets a profit of 2,000 rupees per week while also bartering her wares. She can now afford to hire help to make brooms for the wholesale market. Her small cottage industry business has enabled Laxmi to school her kids and put her grandchildren through university. This dynamic and enterprising woman has also built a house for her daughter and herself and another for her son.

Behind Laxmi's wide smile is a strong and determined person who was able to change and steer the course of her life sans an education, armed with only a traditional skill. She has also addressed over 100,000 rural households over community radio to share her business story. Laxmi says: 'Because of local banks which give women access to finance, they can develop and grow their businesses.'

Through the radio programme women get to learn about the market. The community radio also provides women with a platform to present their traditional skills like folk songs and poetry. Laxmi has also sung her original songs on air several times. She inspired many women from her village to do the same. 'This was the happiest moment of my life. I sang in the studio and was heard by thousands of people.'

Laxmi jokes about retiring soon and happily hopes that when that day comes she would be able to travel in her own car with her own driver to visit her grandchildren. In the meantime, Laxmi continues to ignite a spark in other women and sweep them off their feet.

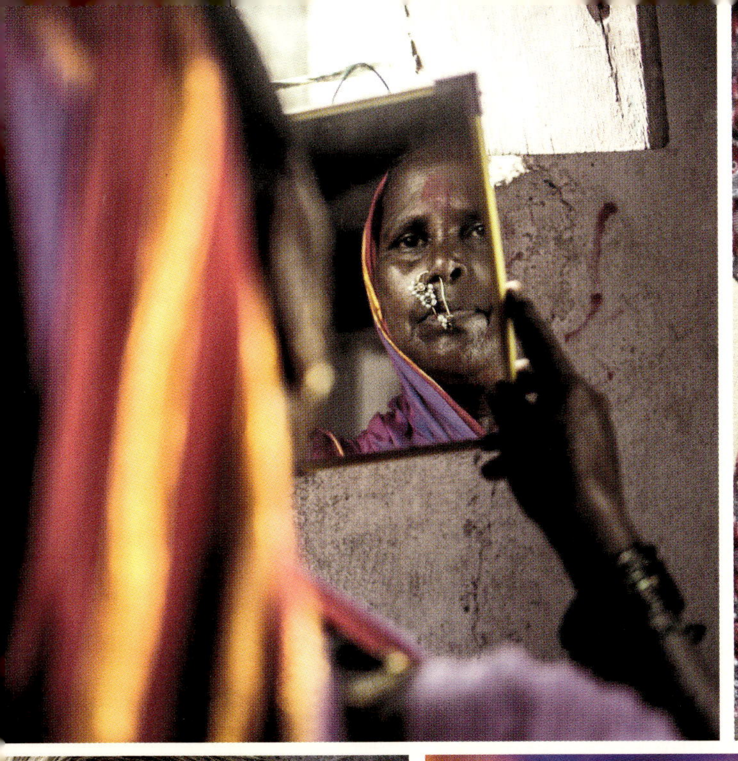

Lakshmi

Survivor

Didn't let an acid attack break her spirit

It feels just like water at first touch. Then in seconds the liquid penetrates deep down into the second layer of skin corroding tissues, muscles, bones and even the organs. Its historic name is 'oil of vitriol', and is commonly known as the 'king of acids'. Easily available at many neighbourhood corner stores for as little as twenty rupees, this lethal, hazardous acid is used in car batteries, fertilizers, and wastewater treatment. Globally, it is also misused as a weapon to attack and violate women.

Lakshmi, a young girl, often admired her reflection in the mirror as most teenage girls do. In 2005, she was violated at a bus stop near an elite shopping market in Delhi. 'Out of nowhere, a woman approached me, put her hand on my face and pinned me to the ground. Immediately, the man she was with emptied a glass of acid on me,' recalls Lakshmi. 'The man was my friend's brother whose advances I had ignored. He was thirty-two years old, and I was all of fourteen.'

'I kept screaming for help but nobody would come forward. Everyone ran in the opposite direction. I could feel my flesh burning and I covered my eyes with my arms. That reflex action saved me from losing my vision. Within a few seconds, I had lost my face, my ear had melted off, and both my arms were charred black. I was in a dark place,' she says. Writhing in pain, she was rescued by a politician's driver, who rushed her to a hospital. While recovering in the hospital, Lakshmi learned from her lawyer Aparna Bhatt, that four other girls had been victims of acid attacks. 'My lawyer supported me and advised me to focus on the bigger picture. So in 2006, we filed a public interest litigation (PIL) in the Supreme Court, appealing for a ban on the sale of acid,' she says with admirable gumption. 'I wanted the government to execute a ban but the government looks deeply at the issue only during election time. Do they want to increase the victim head count? There are so many girls who have lost their vision. Their lives are a complete waste now.' Lakshmi attended every court hearing for seven long years. During this period, she underwent seven medical procedures and now needs four more before she qualifies for plastic surgery. For the first five years following her attack, Lakshmi did not dare to step out into the world with her face uncovered. 'Through this traumatic time when my family and I were struggling to come to terms with my situation, my brother contracted tuberculosis and my father passed away. I had lost my job and no one was willing to employ me. Gradually I reached out to other survivors for succour, most of whom had lost their sight and hearing in the attack, and they are the only friends I have today,' says Lakshmi.

In July 2013, the Supreme Court ruled to regulate the sale of acid at retail outlets across the country and fixed a compensation of 3 lakh rupees for the victims. Lakshmi believes, 'The court has given us hope with this verdict and we now want the state governments to implement it.' In the meantime, Lakshmi became associated with Stop Acid Attacks, an NGO which aims to be the 'bridge between survivors and society'. She campaigns actively for the NGO for a small remuneration which she uses to support her sibling and mother.

In her spare time, she likes to sing and sing she does from her soul: battered but not broken. She says, knowingly, 'When people find it difficult to look at me, how can I expect a man to marry me?' Twenty three year-old Lakshmi has braved the past and now braces herself for the future. Time heals...and so will Lakshmi.

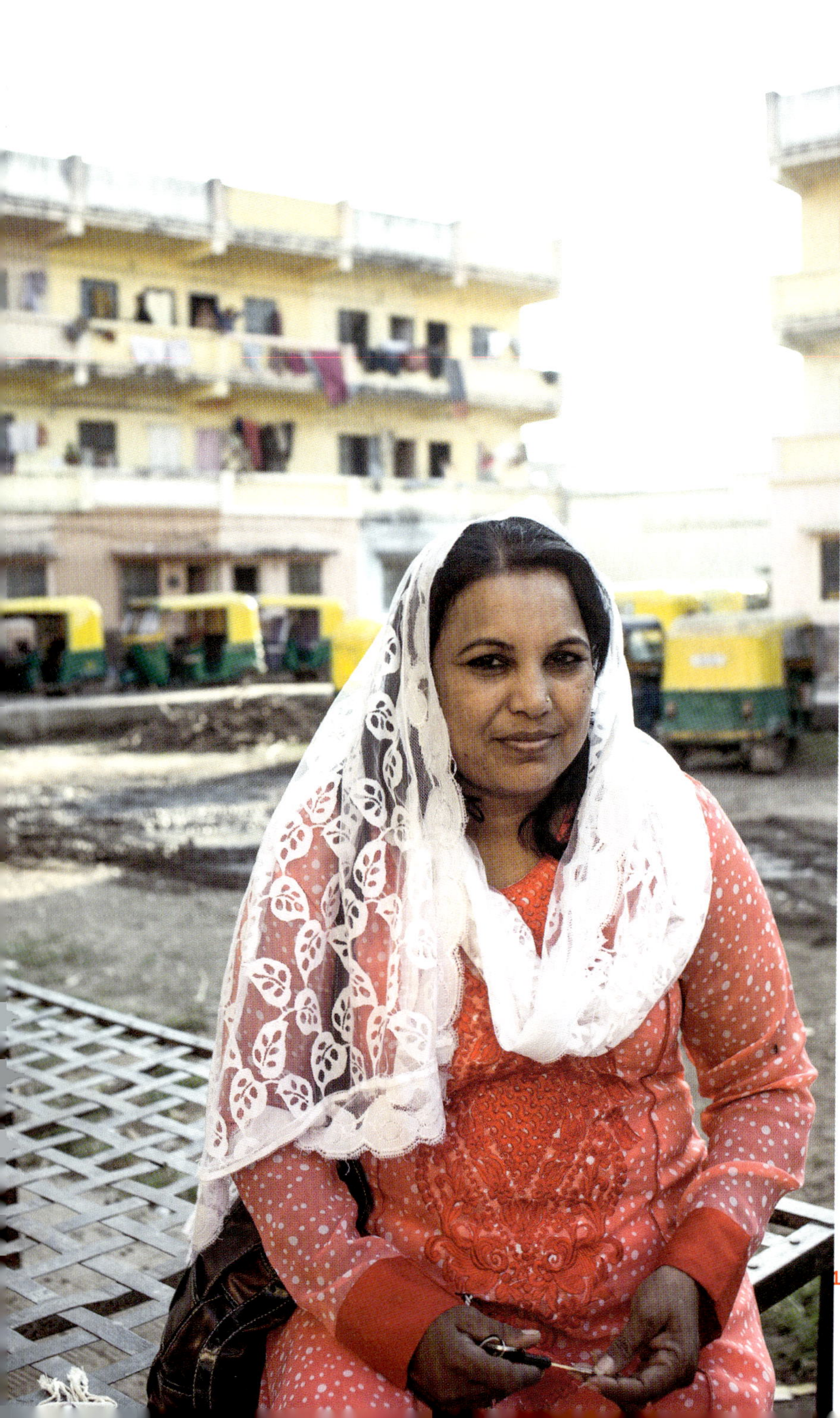

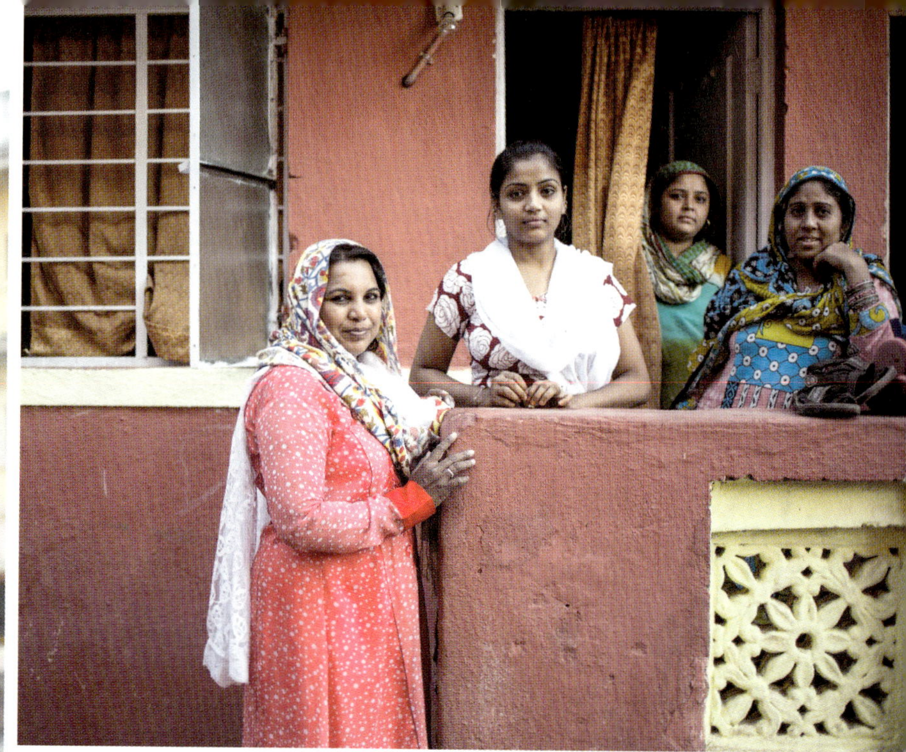

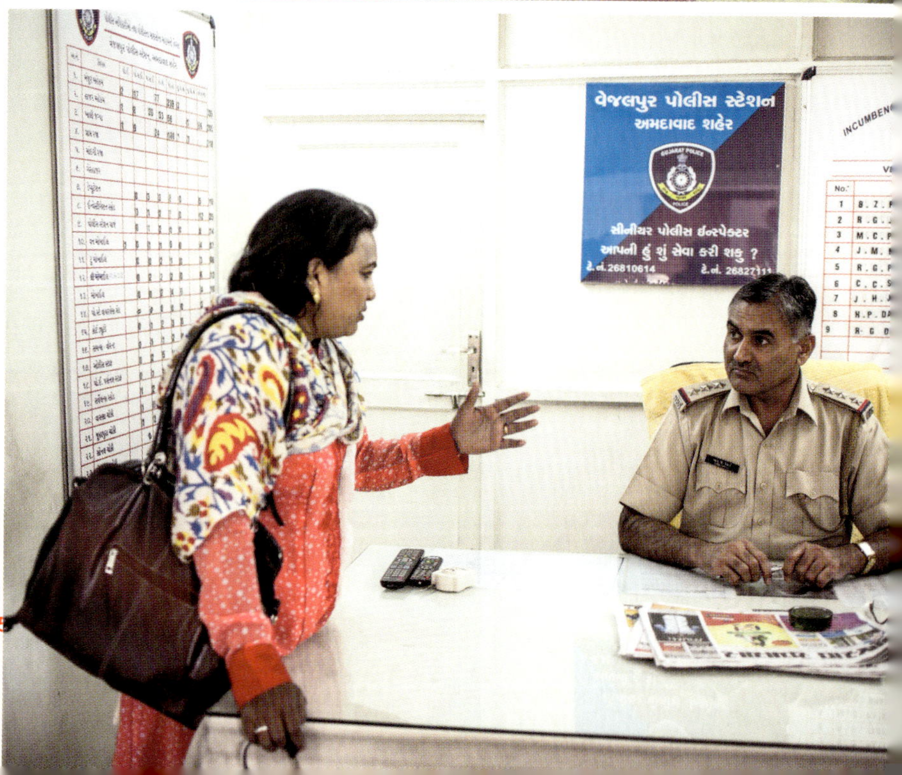

વેજલપુર પોલીસ સ્ટેશન
અમદાવાદ શહેર
સીનીયર પોલીસ ઈન્સ્પેક્ટર
આપની હું શું સેવા કરી શકુ ?
ટે.નં.26810614
ટે.નં. 2682

Noorjehan Dewan

From the frontlines

Coordinator, ANHAD

It is Ahmedabad, 2002. Smoke billows out into the sky as houses and shops burn. Screams of the innocent render through the air. A terrified young woman holds her 6-month-old baby to her chest and sneaks out of a back door. Her husband follows with their two other small children. They run for their lives.

For weeks, this was Noorjehan Dewan's life, as she lived in fear of rioting mobs. Surrounded by anger and hate, yet observing small acts of succour and kindness between the communities shaped her thinking of the future. When things returned to a modicum of normalcy after the riots and she could go back home, some volunteers from an NGO came around asking for clothes and food to help the people in the relief camps. Noorjehan started mobilizing the collection from her vicinity. She then went to a camp herself and was tremendously moved – and thus her journey began.

Noorjehan was not always the confident, brave leader that she is today. 'I was too afraid to go out on my own, even to the bus stop,' she admits. Married off at 18, she had two children in quick succession and her childhood dreams of becoming a lawyer faded away. But then her in-laws encouraged her to study. She joined the Mahila Arts College at Himmatnagar. 'Here I would work and take care of children, husband and in-laws but would study at night. This went on for two years. But I still couldn't complete my third year, I'll always regret it though I shall try to complete it privately some time.'

She also did a computer course. When the Gujarat riots started, she jumped into the fray, helping with relief work, medical aid and more. One of the NGOs noticed her dedication, and trained her in jobs like filing of FIRs, communication skills, and much more.

She eventually joined Shabnam Hashmi's organization, ANHAD (Act Now for Harmony and Democracy) which works on issues related to democracy, secularism, communal harmony, gender equality, women's empowerment, and justice. Her work involved stepping out of her home and her comfort zone, meeting people, visiting police stations; in short, leading from the front on behalf of the victims of communal violence and exploitation, mainly women.

Despite being mocked by neighbours, and on occasion, thrashed by her husband, she stuck it out. She says, 'There was an occasion when we had to accompany young children to Madras (now Chennai) for their schooling since their fathers were arrested under POTA (Prevention of Terrorism Act). But my husband protested. I did not listen to him. A night before leaving for Madras, he beat me terribly but I did not cry. I went to Madras the next day. When I returned he did not speak to me for about six months. That was the turning point for me. It was the last time he ever raised a hand at me.'

Today, she is the coordinator at ANHADs Gujarat office and state convener of the Bharatiya Muslim Mahila Aandolan. She travels to Delhi alone for work and to visit her children who are in college there. She works mainly on relief and rehabilitation of victims, helping them re-establish their lives through vocational training, literacy, and education. Noorjehan explains, 'My dream is to now bring out women of all communities to fight for their cause, to help all those who are ignored, marginalized, and exploited. I want this chain of help to become bigger and better.'

Seema Pandey

Still I rise

District Coordinator, Sakhi Kendra

A young girl runs along the village street, *ghunghat* (veil) covering her face. She knocks on a door and slips inside, where she falls down with a groan. Her family members gather around. Her father picks her up, pulls her veil off and cries out in horror. Her throat is swollen, her blouse torn. She reeks of kerosene and her back is splattered with blood and gashes. 'How could they do this?' he sobs. 'Why didn't you tell us how bad it was?' She says in hoarse voice, 'Close the door, Papa. I don't want the neighbours to see.'

Seema narrates her story of horror and abuse. She was married to a man she had never met. Forced into this marriage himself, her husband would drink and spend nights with other women. He would beat up Seema regularly and even tried to make her sleep with his friends. Her in-laws did not give her food, and once she had to go without water for almost 20 days. Seema was not allowed to speak out or cry. Even her little son was starved sometimes. Her family was not permitted to see her either. She ran away 26 times, and every time her in-laws brought her back, and she went with them meekly. It was a classic case of the battered-wife syndrome, together with the typical Indian bias about her parents' honour being tarnished if she went back to their home. The most surprising part of this whole ordeal is that Seema is a post graduate. As a little girl, she had great ambitions. 'I was always full of restlessness when I saw women around me suffering. I realized that I did not want to be like them. And the only way out was to study. I was inspired by my grandmother, who was a fighter.'

Seema would walk for miles to get books, and travelled on a precarious road via bullock carts or tempos to get to school. 'I started giving tuitions to fund my studies from the time I was in high school. I managed to finish a master's and got a job as a librarian in Lucknow, and later as a Montessori teacher.'

This was when she was married off and her nightmare began. Two years and a heap of abuses later, she finally left. Her husband poured kerosene on her and was about to set her ablaze. 'I just stood there, paralyzed, till a neighbour's 11-year-old child grabbed my hand and asked me to run.' She was traumatised. 'I was so scared, I had no confidence. I could not fill any job application, and would tremble if any one shouted.'

A chance meeting with volunteers of Sakhi Kendra, an NGO, helped her put her life back together. She began to listen to other stories like hers. She resolved, 'I realized I could work on myself, and help other women. I do not want anyone to suffer the way I did.'

With time Seema started travelling to villages in order to create awareness among women of their rights. She got involved with other projects as well – maternal health, women's security, sanitation, hygiene and more. 'People want their women in purdah at home, but they are perfectly all right with sending them out with a *lota* (mug) to relieve themselves in the fields! This is laughable.' Promoted to district coordinator, Seema began to train women on paths to empowerment.

Seema's son is now 20. He is in the navy. 'I wanted to educate him and make him a good, respectful human being. I am so proud of him, now he is all of that, and everyone loves him.' The authorities now know she will not back down in her fight against injustice. 'Now I have the power to change people so that they don't suffer, and get their rights. 'Not all of them are bad,' she says, giving her insight on men.

Sharda Bhati

Former *Devdasi*

Fighting Forced-Prostitution

The women of the Saraniya community never marry. Instead they are pimped out by their menfolk for easy earnings. This practice started when the community was serving the Maharaja many generations ago. But even after independence, when the government gave the villagers land to cultivate, they chose the more convenient option of the *devdasi* system. Moved by the position of women in the community who were merely commodities for trading between their families and brokers, a determined young woman named Sharda Bhati took a stand, and changed everything.

Sharda, 37, knew what love and family support meant. Her parents, although fairly poor, were unqualifiedly supportive of her education. She went to school in Rajasthan and then got married. With a desire to do something constructive in her spare hours, she volunteered with an NGO, Vicharti Jaati Samuday Samarthan Manch (VJSSM).

The organization had decided to intervene in this deep-seated cultural practice of the 100-family-strong Saraniya community, and they chose Sharda to lead the charge. Sharda very soon realized that her task was not going to be simple. The economics of the situation ruled everything. Even the few families who did not want to send their girls into the flesh trade but get them married or educated, were threatened and bullied by the brokers and other villagers, on occasions resulting in the murder of the helpless girls. As soon as they hit puberty, the girls, sometimes as young as 12, were turned into sex workers.

As Sharda investigated the situation further, she saw the cracks in this twisted system. If women were engaged or married, they were not forced to sell their bodies (this had led to a rise in child brides as the lesser of two evils).

'The young people of the community were not keen on this system, they wanted a different life for themselves,' she points out. She and her team began building a rapport with the young boys and girls of the village, enlisting them in her way of thinking. She offered vocational courses for the girls. Taking a principled and firm stand against the brokers, she got the local police on her side. She and her colleagues spoke to families and convinced them that their children deserved more than this barbaric custom.

Sharda, with the help of VJSSM, organized a mass marriage, the first of its kind in Wadia Village. In front of the furious brokers, young people shattered the *devdasi* practice, transforming the course of their lives forever. Over 75 families have broken away from the practice, and they now send their daughters to school. The NGO has also worked to create roads and infrastructure, and provisions of drinking water to the village. The desolate region is now green and vibrant, and rings with the happy voices of those who fought to be free of the horror of its history.

Sharda Bhati's life has been threatened several times. She often gets frustrated with the regressive thinking and fear that she sees in people. But she never gives up fighting. 'I feel proud when I see people leave prostitution and look for an alternate livelihood. And I am also proud to be working in this area and making a difference.' Her children are inspired by her and want to assist their mother in her work when they grow up.

Sua Kalbeliya

Dancing with herself

Kalbelia Dancer

The dancer is a blur of colour, her sinuous moves are snake-like and hypnotic, her *ghunguroos* (anklets) keeping time with the cheers and claps from the mesmerized crowd. As she takes her final bow, her smile is like a beacon, lighting up her eyes. You can tell that this dancer is no ordinary woman. Sua Kalbeliya has fought the odds – odds that were stacked up against her.

Sua, 36, grew up in makeshift camps or *deras* where her tribe, the Kalbeliyas, lived. A nomadic people from Rajasthan, the Kalbeliyas are traditionally snake handlers and poison sellers, considered untouchable by the higher castes. Yet, they had something precious that they held on to – their distinctive performing art form. As a child, Sua was surrounded by the unique dance traditions of her people, handed down over generations, and usually performed recreationally for weddings. Sua's mother never sent her to school, but taught the little girl the sensuous, serpent-like moves of this ancient dance. 'I started learning the dance when I was 7 years old,' says Sua. 'It's in my blood.'

When the Wildlife Act of 1972 banned snake handling, the Kalbeliyas were badly hit. They no longer had a means of livelihood available to them, since this had been their profession for generations. Desperate and with no other option, they fell back on their traditional dance and music in order to make a living – and it was here that Sua's training stood her in good stead. 'Earlier, I thought of it just as a source of income, but when I saw people enjoying my art so much, I came to love it.' The performances of the Kalbeliyas have since become extremely popular, allowing her to earn a living doing something she loves. The tribe also takes pride in its women who are the real bread-winners, while the men handle logistics and play the music.

Sua is one of the best known of the Kalbeliya dancers. Her talent has driven her and her troupe to perform at hundreds of venues, spreading their culture in India and the USA, all over Europe, and in London. 'When I first went out of India, I didn't know how to talk or do much, but now I can get by quite well. I have seen so many wonderful places because of my dance,' she says with pride. 'Before, we used to travel on donkeys; now we travel on flights!' She has delighted audiences with her passion and skill, and basks in the liberation of artistic freedom.

The biggest return, of course, is the financial independence, which she thanks her dancing fervently for. Sua now earns a good amount for every performance, which she invests in educating her children. 'The Kalbeliyas who chose to dance for a living are doing so well. The others, still in the village, live hand-to-mouth, begging for survival. I feel so bad for them – they can only give their children food, whereas my children have a good life.

They wear good clothes, they study, they eat well...' Her children have all learned the dance form, and the older ones sometimes perform with her. 'Recently my older son and daughter went to France. They loved it. I told them; it is because of this dance that you have been able to see the world. Be grateful for it.' As she pirouettes, Sua's tattoos catch one's eye. Her skirt, embroidered with mirror-work, is rich in blacks and reds. Her chunky jewellery clinks and tinkles, just like her laugh when she says, 'It feels incredible to be an artist and a woman.'

Sulekha Ali

As one

Founder, Arzoo

It is impossible to tell that Sulekha Ali, a young Muslim woman, is a survivor of the violent anti-communal riots of 2002 in Gujarat. She speaks with alacrity and wisdom clearly beyond her years. Although Sulekha came out physically unscathed, she still breathes the memory of the horrific plight of children at Shah Alam camp, where she took refuge for six months. It was here that she changed, in more ways than one; her thinking shaped by her interactions with the traumatized children at the camp.

Sulekha recalls vividly, 'I saw horrific scenes in the medical camp where I volunteered to administer first-aid. The children who came in for treatment were anxious to narrate the heinous scenes they had witnessed. They talked about the barbarity with which little girls were violated by their own neighbours, whom they and their parents trusted. Listening to their stories made me feel as if the experiences were my own; I felt as if someone was tearing me up from within.' Sulekha gravitated towards these children. 'There were kids from 15,000 families. They wandered around, disturbed, and I wondered what I could do. So I began playing with them and that's how I connected with them.' Sulekha forged deep bonds with the children and when she left the camp to return home, she realized that she had to start her life over again.

Although Sulekha's trajectory in social work crystallized in Shah Alam Camp, she defined its name and mission when she set off to Bangalore to learn paper craft. 'Arzoo' means desire in Urdu, and the word echoed my sentiment,' she says. She set up an activity centre to teach paper crafts. Curious children from both communities began to saunter in to play carrom and other games. 'Once I had gained their trust, we started enacting children's stories with a social message of unity and communal harmony. Some of these kids were so badly affected that even their games were about enacting riots. They would form groups and pelt stones at each other. This was their game. Their childhood seemed lost and something else had taken over their minds.'

Sulekha realized the need to impart values to these children through education, and she says, 'Riots took place mostly in areas inhabited by low socio-economic groups. An educated society will have a different outlook. I grew up in a home that did not consider education to be important. I went to college on my own initiative and that enabled me to think about teaching.' Arzoo's mission was thus decided with a focus on education, communal harmony, skills training, and income generation. Sulekha and her co-workers began to organize medical camps, conduct workshops for men and women, teach paper making and create cards, lamps, folders, diaries, and bags.

At Arzoo children from both communities observe roza (fasting during Ramadan), celebrate Diwali (the Hindu festival of lights) and reverse ethnic roles in cultural programmes. Sulekha says, 'When Gandhi*ji* called for freedom, everyone joined in without thinking of their religion. Freedom was everybody's concern and need. We need to be human first.'

Sulekha must know that she continues to share, with her children, the most valuable lesson of all: harmony.

OM
MANI
PADME
HUM

Sunita Dhairyam

Queen of the jungle

Founder, Temple Tree Designs

She watches a *dhole*, an Asiatic wild dog, quenching his thirst at a *katte*, a watering hole. She takes a picture in her mind's eye, and returns to her canvas. Round, flat, Filbert, and fan brushes. Burnt sienna, umber, and ochre oil paints. Flowing strokes and jab strokes. She creates a life-like form: a *dhole*. She smiles, delighted with her painting.

Sunita Dhairyam, 50, has a deep love for nature and wildlife that was nurtured by the indelible influence of her grandmother, a wildlife artist, and her aunt, a wildlife photographer. Sunita was unwittingly wired with the same passion. She grew up in Zambia and studied in India; married and worked in Minneapolis, USA as a mural artist. Years passed and faced with the death of her marriage, she longed to return to India. In 1995, she bought a piece of land and set up a solitary home in Mangala village near Bandipur Tiger Reserve. 'My family thought I was crazy. I bought the land purely for my love of wildlife and the view of the Nilgiris. But I had to fight huge battles to survive and to stay. If I had known what challenges lay ahead, I may not have had the courage to live in Bandipur,' she says. It took Sunita a year to build a one-room shelter, her home, on a barren piece of land sans running water and electricity. Her village was also the lair of the then infamous sandalwood bandit, Veerappan. It was a lonely, hostile place for a woman. 'I was perceived as an outsider for a long, long time,' she recalls.

By a divine stroke of luck, officials of the Karnataka Forest Department happened to hear of her art, and commissioned her to paint murals in the Bandipur Safari Lodge cottages. She brought the jungle indoors with larger-than-life wall murals of wild gaur, elephant, leopards, and tigers – she began to make a living. While she aspired to bolster conservation through art, she felt compelled to address health, social, and economic issues amongst the tribals, and in particular the wildlife conflict. Sunita recognized that the 'ecosystem of animals and humans was fragile'. She understood that the livelihood of the villagers was dependent on their scrub cattle whose dung they sold as fertilizer to tea and coffee plantations. Cattle death by wild cats often sparked in retaliation killings. 'No one cared and no forest official conducted any census. Wildlife officials just want the villagers to get out of the forest.'

In 2000, Sunita offered her land to Dr. A.R. Pai, a philanthropist, to set up a free medical clinic. This paved the way, in 2006, for the Mariamma Charitable Trust, founded in collaboration with Dr. Pai and Shree Devi. The trust provides cattle compensation to locals and aims to reduce the human-wildlife conflict, thereby saving endangered species in an eco-sensitive zone. Conceptually, the programme was a novel idea across 15 villages. Monies, however, were short for the implementation. Sunita went back to the drawing board and to her intrinsic talent to finance the trust. She set up Temple Tree Designs to produce clothing, home décor items, paintings, dhurries, and more, all with her signature wildlife motifs. 'We plough back 20 per cent of our earnings to Mariamma Charitable Trust to provide villagers with cattle compensation,' she says. The trust also provides healthcare for the poor, education for talented rural population, and animal birth control for domestic dogs. Her holistic solutions to foster harmony between humans and animals, and to conserve wildlife, come from her resilience, adaptability, creativity, and intelligence. 'We have to share the environment and live in harmony,' she says, 'and to do this people need to jump in and help. Let us try to make a change.'

SAVE
OUR
AND
Mangala Village
Gundlupet Taluk
Chamarajnagar Dist.
Karnataka
Mob : 09449808796
(Bordering
Bandipur National Park)
(Tiger Reserve)

MARIAMMA TRUST
Male/female
Direct sighting
Over 75%
Village

Vijaylaxmi Sharma

Balika Vadhu no more

Fighting Child Marriage

The girl lies sobbing on the floor, her stomach gnawing with hunger. But the eyes in the tear-streaked face hold a glimmer of steel. The door opens and she looks up at her mother standing there. 'I hope you have changed your mind, you stubborn child!' With all her remaining strength, the child shouts, 'No! I will not get married!' She watches grimly as the door shuts and locks behind her mother. This isn't a scene from an Indian soap, but one from the life of Vijaylaxmi Sharma, who held her own against her community's custom of child marriage. Now she is a teacher and is widely known as a crusader against girls getting married off before the legal age of 18. She recently talked a mother out of marrying off her 10 month-old baby.

Forty per cent of all child marriages in the world happen in India, so when the then 13-year-old Vijaylaxmi resisted her parents attempts to marry her off to an older man, it was an uphill task. She asked them to give her a chance to study, and live her own life for a bit before being shackled by the bonds of marriage. Her argument was strengthened by a neighbour, whose 14-year-old daughter had died at childbirth. Another told the story of her child, widowed at the same age, whose life was thus unfortunately but effectively over.

These tragedies allowed Vijaylaxmi's parents to understand how close they had come to losing their own child, and they decided to stand by her. This was not easy – their choice was mocked by the village, and they were ostracized and harassed for it. 'I had a daily argument with myself, between my own beliefs and my love for my family. But I couldn't betray myself and my life. I knew I was worth much more,' she says. Once she had her parents behind her, Vijaylaxmi decided to pursue her other dream – to go to college. She was a bright student who consistently did well at school. Her teachers saw her potential and her ambition. They spoke to her parents, recommending that she be allowed to study and choose a career for herself.

In the meantime, something else happened. One day, as Vijaylaxmi was settling down to do her homework, there was a knock on the door. A pretty 15-year-old girl walked in hesitantly. She wanted Vijaylaxmi's help in convincing her parents to put off her marriage for a few years, so she could study. Vijaylaxmi went with her, and thus started her new journey. 'I've shown people it can be different, they just need to see there's another way,' she says happily.

Now, every so often, Vijaylaxmi, accompanied by her two brothers, or with a group of young female volunteers, visits homes of girls whom she has heard are about to be married off before their time. She engages with the parents of the girls, and dissuades them from making this big mistake, using herself as an example of what their daughters can achieve, only if they are given wings. Her success rate is higher than you might think!

Vijaylaxmi is doing her master's and preparing for her B.Ed. Her work against child marriage continues, helping countless young girls acquire a life beyond child marriage and its disastrous consequences. 'Taking a stand against child marriage is something even boys will not do. What I have achieved as a girl makes my parents proud. I, too, am proud of what I have achieved on this long, hard road,' she says. She wants to travel to other parts of the country to spread this message. What about marriage now? Yes, she says, she would certainly like that – but happily, it will be to someone she chooses, and when she chooses.

The **Team**

Vodafone Foundation, India (Left to Right):
Ritika Agrawal, Rohit Adya (seated), Madhu Singh Sirohi, and Monika Adlakha

The Vodafone Foundation

Vodafone Foundation in India is combining skills, resources and funding to build a brighter future for people who are currently unable to fulfill their potential. We recognize the power of mobile technology to address some of India's most pressing challenges and use it to encourage innovation, share knowledge and improve lives. We focus our work on areas of greatest need and at scale. We seek to empower women so that they can compete on an equal footing, to reach rural areas and support the people living there, and to provide new opportunities for education.

Rohit Adya

A visionary, compassionate leader, and strong advocate of sustainability, Rohit likes to settle for nothing but the best. His vast experience and understanding of diverse functions including business strategy, operations, corporate social responsibility, and sales and marketing have always helped him see the bigger picture. A strategist and an achiever, he has consistently delivered results in his 34-year-long career. A strong believer in women's empowerment, he is of the view that a man's world is incomplete without a women. Rohit echoes this respect for women by actively supporting the empowerment of womankind.

Madhu Singh Sirohi

An avid cinema enthusiast, Madhu loves to spend time with her family, her books, and her dog. She has been associated with the world of education and corporate social responsibility for over 17 years, and has also authored several educational books. A strong advocate of women empowerment, she firmly believes that women with great potential often get marginalized due to lack of support – financial, familial, educational or emotional. She has been working to address some of the nation's most pressing challenges, and use the power of mobile technology to make a difference.

Monika Adlakha

A writer, *musafir*, and a self-confessed foodie, Monika Adlakha has an insatiable passion for writing, photography, and travel. A noted media-person, she has written extensively on diverse subjects including, technology, films, food, travel, and books for leading publications like *Hindustan Times*, *Mid Day* and *Times of India*. In her current 'corporate' avatar, she's a content strategist and communication specialist who likes having things perfect on paper. Her career can be traced to demonstrate a penchant for capturing the more human side of corporates.

Nivedita Samanta

Passionate about social development, endurance, running, and cooking, Nivedita Samanta is a dynamic individual who thrives in fast paced, engaging, and diverse settings. Currently working at the Vodafone Foundation in India with communications as her forte, Nivedita has worked with the New York State Department Attorney General's office, at Ernst & Young LLP, USA and the British charity the Duke of Edinburgh's Award in India. She strives to be a wizard multi-tasker at work, while training as an athlete, and living as a young woman.

Ritika Agrawal

Ritika Agrawal is confident, fun, generous, and a true adventure enthusiast. An intrepid traveller, her explorations have taken her off the beaten path in India, Europe, and beyond. She enjoys spending time with her DSLR and watching Rafael Nadal hit that perfect shot every single time. For Ritika, the stint in the development world started with voluntary involvement in a Cancer awareness campaign. Since then, she has been passionate about empowering women and youth. Ritika has worked as a business analyst, and is excited to apply her for-profit business analysis knowledge to the non-profit sector.

Anusha Yadav Photographer

Anusha Yadav is a visual researcher & archivist, photographer, and a publication designer. She graduated from National Institute of Design, Ahmedabad in 1997. Her photographs have featured in international and national publications and exhibited at several galleries across India, Austria, USA, and South Africa. In 2010, Anusha founded Indian Memory Project – the world's first online visual and narrative based archive. The project traces a personal history of the Indian subcontinent via photographs found in personal archives. Anusha is an INK fellow, 2011; a L'Oreal Paris *Femina* Women Achiever's award winner, 2013; and recipient of the 'Honorary Mention' at Prix Ars Electronica, 2013.

Ashima Narain Photo Editor

Photographer, film-maker, and the former photo editor for *National Geographic Traveller India*, Ashima Narain has worked on subjects that have sent her wading through mudflats in search of flamingos, climbing sail masts mid-sea, and driving vintage cars. She has twice been nominated for a Green Oscar, and been the recipient of the Ramnath Goenka Wildlife Photographer of the Year 2006 and the Commonwealth Photographer for Asia in 2004. Ashima's work has been published in the coffee table book, *Dining with the Maharajas*, and magazines such as *Vanity Fair*, *Vogue*, *GQ*, *Elle* and *Marie Claire*.

Aparna Jaykumar Photographer

Aparna was a student of art history, silver photography, and ancient Greek literature at the Aegean Center for the Fine Arts in Italy and Greece. Her work has been exhibited at a host of places including the Aegean Center in Paros, Lincoln Center in New York City, Villa Borghese in Rome, Art Bazis in Budapest. She has been published in *Inge Morath Magazine*, *Le Journal de la Photographie*, *Travel+Leisure*, CNNgo.com, the *Sunday Guardian*, and *Caravan* among others. She founded the Bombay Photo Club , and teaches photography at Sophia College, Mumbai.

Eisha Chopra Book Designer

Eisha is a designer, actor, writer, and teacher. She studied Communication Design at Parsons School of Design; filmmaking at Tisch School of Arts, New York University; and screenwriting at London Film Academy. She is also currently visiting faculty at ISDI, Parsons Mumbai. She has created several books, brands, and short films and feature scripts; and her work has been featured extensively in press and television. She has an infinite curiosity for any medium that tells a story, and a work philosophy that is simple, clean, and beautiful.

Karen Dias Photographer

Karen Dias is a Mumbai-based photojournalist with a special interest in political, social, and environmental issues affecting ethnic and tribal communities around the world. She spent four years working as a news photographer for Gulf News based in the UAE. Her work has been published in *Outlook Traveller, Forbes Middle East, Al Jazeera, Harper's Bazaar Arabia*, the *Sunday Guardian*, the *Washington Post*, etc. She is an avid traveller, a martial arts enthusiast, and speaks rudimentary French and Turkish.

Kavita Chopra Dikshit Photographer

Kavita studied sociology at St. Xavier's College, followed by a post-graduate diploma in mass communications from Sophia College. She completed her master's in television production in Pittsburgh, and subsequently worked with CNN at their international headquarters. She moved to Delhi in 1989, where she ran a successful film production company for a few years before moving to an assignment in advertising. She finally set up a full-service graphic design studio, Red Design Company in New Delhi in 2007. She specializes in portrait photography and her preferred genre is black & white portraits.

Mansi Midha Photographer

Mansi Midha is a Delhi-based photographer who moonlights as an editor and curator to her friends and colleagues. She has a background in communication design and a certificate in photojournalism & documentary photography from the International Center of Photography. When not photographing, Mansi remains true to her passion by involving herself in various administrative and educational roles within the photographic community.

Ruchika Chanana Writer

Ruchika is a writer and editor. She has written short stories, features, non-fiction books and screenplays, among other things. She runs Wordsetc., a content/copy/ideas resource. Ruchika has also been a theatre practitioner and television producer.

Tanya Luther Writer

Tanya has developed and taught an 'Emotional Intelligence' programme, and worked as a school psychologist. Her book *Climate Change* was released by Al Gore and R.K. Pachauri. She has developed environmental comics, and her book, *See you Tomorrow*, was selected for libraries of 1100 schools. Tanya plays the piano, dances the tango, and is a doting mother.

Roli Books (Left to Right):
Saloni Vaid, Rayman Gill-Rai, Priya Kapoor (seated), Neelam Narula, and Neharika Gupta

Neelam Narula

Born in Delhi and brought up in various cities around India, thanks to her father, an officer in the Indian Air Force, Neelam is an avid reader, who starts her day by reading at least two newspapers from the first page to last, including obituaries. She is interested in the genre of fiction and contemporary Indian history. She loves life and work, and spends the best part of her day with her six-year-old son. Editing the stories featured in this book has made her more understanding and appreciative of the incredible spirit of women.

Saloni Vaid

A visual researcher and editor, she is passionate about photography and art. A mass communications graduate with a diploma in journalism, she started her career as a photo researcher and has worked for various publishing houses including Harper Collins, Capstone, Heinemann, Scholastic, and Oxford University Press. She has an extensive knowledge of image libraries – both rare and internationally acclaimed. When not writing about herself in the third person, she enjoys travel, movies, and shopping with her sister. After reading about these women, and undertaking extensive photo-coordination on this project, she truly believes it's a 'woman's world'.

Rayman Gill-Rai

Rayman is a writer/editor based in the Capital. She has worked on this book as an editor and project coordinator. Having grown up in tea gardens located in the remote corners of the country, she studied at various formal and informal schools. With degrees in English Literature, journalism, and film production, she has worked at the *Caravan* and the *Times of India*. Newly-married, she has just started to learn the art of striking a balance between home and work, and seeks inspiration from the women featured in this book.

Neharika Gupta

Neharika has a fanatical love for the written word. A student of English Literature and an art enthusiast, she has had hands on exposure to photography, film direction and appreciation. After short-lived affairs with television and advertising, she has now decided to pursue books. As an editor, she aims to internalize all her learning and write a bestseller before she turns 30. She describes editing *Women of Pure Wonder* as 'an intensely empowering yet humbling experience'.

Priya Kapoor

Born into a family of publishers, books are in Priya's DNA. She feels the best part of the job is the people she meets – everyone has a story to tell, and she loves hearing them. She is passionate about design and textiles and if she wasn't in publishing, she would have been a curator at a museum. Working as an editor, coordinator, and project manager on this book has reaffirmed her belief that only an all-woman team could have pulled off such a mammoth task so meticulously in such a short time!

Photo Credits

Anusha Yadav
Hasina Anand (56)
Indira Hinduja (122, 124-125)
Indu Shahani (60)
Meera Sanyal (106)
Priya Dutt (96)
Safeena Husain (69)
Sangita Tribhuvan (138)
Vijaya Patsala (44)
Zarina Screwvala (50)

Aparna Jayakumar
Anita Kumbhar (18, 20-21, 175)
Chingutai Jadhav (117)
Fehmida Malik (118)
Godavari Dange (90)
Laxmi Lokhande (10-11, 145-147)
Meeratai Umbre (129)
Mittal Patel (93-95)
Nandini Lohar (23-25)
Neera Nundy (28)
Noorjahan Kaladigi (98)
Noorjehan Dewan (150)
Priyanshi Somani (66)
Renuka Dehatonde (15, 133-135)
Dr. (Capt.) Ritu Rajkishore Biyani (top left) (137)
Saberaben A. Ghanchi (105)
Sanjeevani Mali (72, 74-75)
Sharda Bhati (155)
Shobha Raut (38)
Sulekha Ali (161-163)
Trishala Dangare (41)
Vanita Pise (31-33)
Vidya Joshi (79-81)

Karen Dias
Asma Rahim (114)
Nandini Sardesai (70)
Pinky Devi (103)
Sunita Dhairyam (164, 166-167)
Usha Prajapati (76)

Kavita Chopra Dikshit
Shahnaz Husain (43)
Priti Paul (35)
Aruna Roy (89)

Mansi Midha
Anita Rana (85)
Bimla Devi (142)
Chhavi Rajawat (87)
Kshama Metre (126)
Gulafsha Khan (55)
Kanku Bai (121)
Lakshmi (149)
Laxmi Gautam (59)
Nirmala Misra (65)
Norti Bai (101)
Pooja Bansal (62)
Ranno Devi (131)
Rekha (36)
Seema Pandey (153)
Sheelu Singh Rajput (46)
Sister Mariola (109)
Sua Kalbelia (157-159)
Sunita Kasera (110)
Vijaylakshmi (49)
Vijaylaxmi Sharma (168)

Other sources
Biocon Biochemicals Limited (26)
Dr. (Capt.) Ritu Rajkishore Biyani (137)
Shyam Benegal (12)